W9-BWD-331

The Night
the Whole Class
Slept Over

Other Clarion novels by Stella Pevsner:

How Could You Do It, Diane?
Sister of the Quints
Me, My Goat, and My Sister's Wedding
Cute Is a Four-Letter Word
And You Give Me a Pain, Elaine
A Smart Kid Like You
Keep Stompin' Till the Music Stops
I'll Always Remember You . . . Maybe
Lindsay, Lindsay, Fly Away Home

• • • STELLA PEVSNER

The Night
the Whole Class
Slept Over

CLARION BOOKS • NEW YORK

Clarion Books
a Houghton Mifflin Company imprint
215 Park Avenue South, New York, NY 10003
Text copyright © 1991 by Stella Pevsner
All rights reserved.
For information about permission to reproduce selections
from this book, write to Permissions, Houghton Mifflin
Company, 2 Park Street, Boston, MA 02108.
Printed in U.S.A.

Library of Congress Cataloging-in-Publication Data
Pevsner, Stella.
    The night the whole class slept over / by Stella Pevsner.
        p. cm.
        Summary: Eleven-year-old Dan, whose artist parents have kept him moving around all his
    life, fears he will lose the friends he has made at his new school, until the class sleepover
    coincides with a bad winter storm.

        ISBN 0-89919-983-6
        [1. Friendship—Fiction.   2. Schools—Fiction.   3. Family life—Fiction.   4. Artists—
    Fiction.]   I. Title.
    PZ7.P44815Ni   1991
    [Fic]—dc20   91-6575
                                                                                          CIP
                                                                                           AC

BP 10 9 8 7 6 5 4 3 2 1

DEFIANCE PUBLIC LIBRARY

'APR 1 3 1993 c.3s

J
P

Doubleday 15.00 4/93

*With love, for Stuart, Marian,
Charles, Nita, and Barbara*

Contents

1

Arrival at Lake Lorraine

"Oh, look!" Mom suddenly cried out. "It's Lake Lorraine!" She turned from the front seat of the car. "Dan, do you see it?"

"I see it," I said. What I thought was, *Whoop-de-do, another biggie.* How many lakes, rivers, and streams had I seen so far on this trip east?

"Martha, baby," Mom now said to my two-year-old sister, "see the lake, honey? That's Mommy's lake, the one she grew up on."

Her saying that made me visualize a raft with Mom on it, growing bigger and bigger. "You didn't actually grow up *on* the lake," I said.

Mom ignored me, as she usually did when I was being literal, instead of artistic . . . like her.

"And now, Martha," she said to my sister in her seat between Mom and Dad, "we're going to Grandma and Grandpa's house. Won't that be wonderful?"

I don't know why she bothered asking. Two-year-old Martha refused to talk. I knew she could, because I'd come upon her one time blabbing away to her stuffed animals. This was before she bopped them for being bad.

Now Mom turned to Dad. "Honey, just follow this road

as it winds around the lake, and we'll soon come to The Poplars."

"I remember," Dad said. "It's been a while, though."

He wasn't kidding. We hadn't been to my grandparents' home since I was about eight, and I'm eleven now. I could still picture it, though. Their house was really big, with two stories and lots of curves and niches. So big, in fact, that they ran a bed-and-breakfast place in the summer for tourists who came to spend time at the lake.

Now, in November, there weren't any tourists around. There'd be plenty of room in my grandparents' home for us to stay. I wondered how long we'd be staying.

It made me sick, the way we were always moving around. It wasn't that we were homeless. I mean, we could afford a place to live. My dad didn't seem to have any trouble finding a job teaching art, and my mom made bucks selling her paintings. It was just my parents . . . all right, my mother mostly . . . always had this dream of finding the ideal place to live.

As we drove by birch trees lining the lake, I counted off the places we'd lived in the last few years. There was some art colony in the East when I was about eight and an artists' paradise (hah!) in New Mexico where last Christmas they'd strung strings of chilies on cactus plants for holiday decorations. Where else? Oh, yeah, I mustn't forget that place south of San Diego where Mom wouldn't let me learn to surf.

Lately, we'd been in Chicago. We went there so Mom could get back on good terms with an art gallery that had lost track of her. One day Mom hauled over a bunch of oils and watercolors she'd done in the last couple of years. The gallery director said they should sell. Art collectors, she told Mom, were into Southwest motifs these days.

I liked being in Chicago because Dad took me to some great museums, but I got tired of people asking how come I wasn't in school. What could I say? I was tempted to tell one old lady who questioned me that I was a child genius who had already finished college. She looked like she might be a retired teacher, though, so I went for the truth . . . we were on our way to Wisconsin.

I didn't tell her what was coming after that because there was no point. Anyway, just thinking about it made me queasy.

*

I got kind of used to the subject of what we were going to do next after being at my grandparents' house for a couple of weeks.

At first they refused to believe that my mom (it was her idea) really intended to move us to a log cabin up near the Canadian border. I didn't blame them for not believing. It certainly was a "crackpot" idea, and I'm directly quoting my grandfather.

"I don't see why you're both being so hostile," my mother said one time. "Just because we want to live as nature intended."

"Nature intended," my grandmother repeated. "Rachel, you always did have far-out ideas, but this one tops them all." She put some knives in a drawer and slammed it.

"How do you expect to make a living, off in the woods somewhere?"

"If you mean have all the luxuries that people like you . . ."

"What I mean is food on the table, heat in the house."

"Mother," my mom said, "we've always been able to provide for our children. And they'll be lots better off, living a natural life, rather than being caught up in . . . in trashy TV, video games, VCPs."

"VCRs," I corrected.

"See?" my mom said. "Dan knows all about that electronic garbage, even though we've tried to educate him about—"

"Speaking of education," my grandfather chimed in, "where do you intend to find decent schools for the kids, up in the frozen North?"

My mom, caught off guard, flushed a little. "There must be a good school somewhere." She pushed her hair back. "Or else . . . well, I might decide to teach Dan and Martha myself."

My grandparents didn't say anything, but I guessed they were thinking what I was: *Abandon ship . . . torpedo ahead!* My mom is smart enough in the fields of art, music, and literature, but you can forget science and math. When I ask for help in those subjects, she says something like, "Oh sweetie, I'll have to read the text. Do something else in the meantime." My grandmother could tutor me much better. She's a school superintendent, and seems to know a lot about everything.

After that particular conversation, I wandered into the

living room to watch television. I figured it might be my last chance to do it during my formative years.

*

As the days went on, I noticed my dad getting antsy. At dinner one night, he grumbled about the time we were wasting. "I didn't think it would take so long to find leads on a log cabin," he said. "Here it's November, and if we don't get settled soon—"

"Oh, honey," Mom said, "if you can't connect with a college up there in time, you could always go back to your painting."

"Would you rather be in a classroom, teaching?" Grandpa asked.

When Dad nodded, Mom smiled and said, "He misses having all those pretty girls falling in love with him."

This was news to me. "Why do they fall in love?"

Mom tweaked Dad's cheek. "Because he's so sweet-natured, and so blond and blue-eyed and good-looking."

I'd never thought of it before, but just then I was sorry I had dark hair and eyes, like Mom. Did that mean no girls would fall for me?

"What about Martha, here?" Grandma Alice asked. "The poor child won't have any little playmates. The way you've hauled her around from place to place, it's no wonder she doesn't talk. She probably doesn't even know where she is half the time."

"She'll talk when she's ready," Mom said. "Won't you, pumpkin?"

Martha just scowled.

In my opinion, my sister would talk when she had something to say. As for playmates, what about me? I hadn't had a friend I could keep in my whole lifetime.

Right then I decided to get my grandmother alone sometime and ask her to enroll me in school, right here in Lake Lorraine. Maybe if I got involved, my folks would let me stay behind when they moved, at least until next summer.

I spent the rest of the meal thinking of how great it would be to live in this house with my loving grandparents, who acted like normal people. They had sense enough to eat regular food instead of that mangy health stuff Mom was always shoving at us. They had friends of all kinds instead of just artists. And probably best of all, they had a really great TV set with a remote control. So far neither of them had told me my mind would grow mold if I sat there staring at the screen.

Could I possibly talk my folks into letting me stay? I knew a direct approach wouldn't work; Mom was very strong-willed. But then so was my grandmother. If I could get Grandma Alice on my side, I might have a sporting chance. It was worth a try. Even if it just meant going to school and hanging around some kids my age for a while, until we moved, it would be worth it.

Yep, I'd do it. I'd ask Grandma as soon as possible.

2

Felix—What a Guy!

It worked! All I did was tell Grandma Alice that I felt a paralysis creeping into my mind. And I added that if I didn't get to school pretty soon, my whole brain might become ossified.

She quirked an eyebrow as if to let me know I was overdoing it, but she said, "All right, Dan, I'll see what we can arrange."

She didn't waste any time talking to Mom. I was in the living room and had the TV on but the sound turned down. I could hear Grandma out in the kitchen saying ". . . It's just ridiculous for him to kill time like this when he should be in school," and so on.

After a while I heard Mom coming toward me, so I eased up the sound on the TV and acted interested in a commercial about lower-back pain.

"Honey," she said, sitting on the floor beside me, "I really hate to see you waste time like this watching that junk on TV."

"I have nothing else to do," I told her. "I don't know any kids here, and even if I did, they're all in school."

"Well, how would you like to go to school, too?"

"Really?" I said, widening my eyes. "Don't you want to teach me anymore?"

"Oh, Dan, I'd love to, but I've got to free up some time. You know, it takes a while to find a place to live, and it seems there aren't all that many log cabins to choose from."

"Oh," I said. "Then maybe you ought to give up on the idea."

"Not a chance," Mom said, rising to her feet. "I'm determined. There's the perfect little place for us somewhere up north, and I'm going to locate it."

As she was leaving the room, I called out, "When do I start school?"

"Tomorrow, I guess. Your grandmother said she'd take care of enrolling you."

So I landed in sixth grade the very next day. That grandma of mine doesn't mess around.

.

The thing I've always dreaded about being the new kid is the *introduction*. Teachers never just ease you into the class and let kids gradually notice that you're there. Oh, no. They haul you up in front of the room and let everyone stare at you.

This teacher was fairly casual, though. With a hand on my shoulder, she said, "Class, this is Dan Wakefield." That's all. It was an enormous relief that she didn't ask me to tell about myself, the way some teachers do. So it was just a few seconds that I had to stand there, looking at the kids while they looked back at me. Still, I noticed a red-haired guy raising and lowering his eyebrows a few times while crossing his eyes. Either he'd practiced that a lot or he was naturally talented, because later on at home I tried to do that trick but couldn't.

I also noticed, as I walked toward my desk, the prettiest girl I'd ever seen, and she was smiling at me. I almost stumbled. Seated, all I could see of the girl was the back of her head. She had long, shiny, dark hair held in place by a blue band.

I found out, when the teacher called on her in science class, that the girl's name was Amanda. *Amanda.* I hoped that smile she'd given me wasn't just out of politeness.

You're in class now, so pay attention, I told myself. I was out of training, but I forced myself to concentrate on what the teacher was telling us.

Suddenly a folded note landed *kerplunk* on my desk. I glanced around, but everyone was looking at either the teacher or the science book.

All the note said was, *"You're sitting in B.J.'s place."*

What was that supposed to mean? If B.J.—whoever he was—had moved away, it wasn't his seat anymore. If he was out sick, well, I'd just get another seat when he came back.

When we got out of that class and were moving down the hall to the next, the red-haired kid who'd crossed his eyes before came along beside me.

"Hi," he said. "How ya doin'? My name's Felix. Felix Drake."

"Hi. I'm . . . well . . . I guess you know."

"Where do you live?"

Oh, boy. Someday that was going to be an embarrassing

question. *We live in an old log cabin with no floors, furnace, air conditioning, TV . . . !* "We're staying at my grandparents' house. For a while."

"Where's that?"

"Over on Lakeview. They own The Poplars. It's a bed-and-breakfast place for tourists . . . in the summer."

"Oh, neat! I've always wanted to see the inside of that house. I guess it's about the biggest in town."

"Yeah." Somehow, I felt a little proud.

"Did you get to pick out any bedroom you wanted?"

"Just about."

"Really neat. Could I come over sometime and see the layout?"

"Sure."

We were at the door of the math room by now, and again I was assigned a seat. And again, a note landed on my desk. This time it said, "You're going to catch it from B.J.!" I looked around. Some kid in a striped T-shirt gave me an evil grin.

Who was this B.J., anyway? Some big, tough guy? I hoped I wasn't going to have to fight someone. If I did and Mom found out about it, I could kiss going to school good-bye.

After school Felix asked me if I wanted to go over to his house. I told him I had to check in at home . . . my grandparents' home.

"Okay," he said. "Then I'll go there. If you don't mind."

"Sure," I said. I was thinking, *Wow, I've made a friend the very first day of school!*

We took a shortcut through town. Felix stopped in front

of a video store. "Hey, look, new releases!" he said. "Let's go rent a couple. My folks have a charge here. We can watch them at your place."

"Felix, we don't have a VCR."

He looked at me with his pale blue eyes, forehead wrinkled. "You *what?*"

I felt like an alien. "You see . . ." I hesitated.

"Oh, right," he said then. "You're at your grandparents', and they're old and out of it."

I nodded, feeling like a coward. I should have gone on to confess my parents didn't have a VCR either, but I didn't want to come off totally weird. This kid was the only friend I had at the moment.

"Oh, well," Felix said, turning from the window. "I can always rent them later. I ought to spend the time at my computer, anyway."

I didn't want to get into computer talk.

"You think it'll be okay if I look around The Poplars?" he said as we came to the street by the lake and began walking toward the house.

"Sure, it'll be fine." I couldn't see why he'd be all that interested. It was a nice house . . . big . . . but here was a kid with a VCR and possibly a computer right in his own home! How could a big old house even try to compete with that?

As we neared The Poplars, I happened to shove my hands in my pockets and felt the notes. "Felix," I said, "who's B.J.?"

Felix made a *huh* sound deep in his throat. "Please don't start with me about B.J.," he said.

"Could you tell me what the initials stand for?"

"Bad Joke." I gave him a look. "No, actually, Billie Jo."

"What's wrong with him?"

"Everything. And it's a *her*, not a *him*. The name's spelled the girl way, with an *ie* instead of a *y*."

"How come she's not in school?" I asked.

"She's got chicken pox."

"Chicken pox?" I gave a little laugh. "Come on, really? The itchy, spotty sickness?"

"Yeah." Felix grinned. "I kind of like to think of old B.J. scratching away, just like a chicken."

I said, "Some kid at school threw a couple of notes on my desk. He said I was going to catch it. I didn't know he meant chicken pox."

"Yeah. I saw Joe throw those notes. He has the mentality of a mudguard. As though anyone would be stupid enough to believe you could pick up a disease from a desk!"

"That's stupid, all right," I said, not wanting to admit even to myself that just for a moment I'd thought it might be possible.

We were turning into our driveway when a dynamo ran around the corner and charged toward us. It was my baby sister, Martha, wearing only shoes and socks and underwear even though it was cold outside. For a two-year-old, Martha can be rough. I reached down to grab her or she would have plowed right into my legs.

"Hey, take it easy," I said as Martha twisted and tried to bite my wrist. I held both of her arms over her head and kept back out of her reach. "Where's Mommy?" I asked her. I was wasting my breath, of course, since Martha wouldn't talk.

Felix eyed my sister, keeping well away from her kicking legs. "Does . . . that . . . belong to you?" he asked.

"Yeah, I have to admit—cut it out, Martha!"

"How come she's not—almost not dressed?" Felix asked as we made our way to the back of the house, the kid kicking for all she was worth.

"Don't ask me."

Mom was coming out of the back screened-in porch when we got there. "Oh, you little savage!" she said. "I turn my back for one minute and look what happens." She took hold of Martha. The kid was at least smart enough not to maul, bruise, or bite my parents.

"Mom, this is Felix," I said. "He's in my class."

"How nice," Mom said. She shifted Martha to her other arm and reached out to shake hands. "Come on inside, boys. It's chilly out here." She went in, cuddling Martha and murmuring something about her being naughty. *Naughty?* Beastly, that's what my sister is.

After they had gone, Felix said, "She's really young for a mother."

"Young? She's the regular age." It was probably Mom's long hair and her way of dressing that made Felix think so.

"I hope that when I get married my wife will stay young-looking. But she'll have to be smart, too. That may leave out both Shirley and Traci."

"Who are they?" I opened the door to the screened-in back porch.

"Two girls I like. Who do you like?" Felix followed me across to the kitchen door.

Amanda, I thought. "It's too soon to tell," I said.

When we entered the house, Felix stood and stared. "Wow, what a big kitchen! And a stove-stove! Is something baking there in the oven?"

"I guess. Yeah. It's probably a roast."

"Imagine. And it's only . . ." Felix looked at his watch. It was loaded with dials, hands, slots. ". . . Four thirty. What a trip!"

I was beginning to wonder if Felix had both oars in the water. I mean, all this excitement over a stove . . . a roast?

"Could we see some of the other rooms? If that's okay?"

"Sure." I led the way. "Here's the dining room."

Felix's eyes opened wide and he shook his head. "A genuine dining room table. Must seat . . ."

"About twelve, maybe fourteen, if both leaves are in the table."

"Amazing."

We went on through the downstairs rooms. Felix took the living room with its fireplace in stride but went crazy over the now-closed-off sun room next to the living room. I opened the door so he could look around. "This is where the tourists have breakfast," I told him. "In the summer, when they stay here. It's closed off when the weather turns cool, to save heat."

"That's just so neat," Felix said. He looked up the tall, winding staircase. "I don't suppose . . ."

"Come on up," I said, leading the way.

I showed him the big bathroom off the main hall and

let him peek into my grandparents' and my parents' bedrooms, and the guest rooms.

"Just look at those antiques!" Felix exclaimed. "I know the furniture's safe, but don't tourists swipe the smaller things?"

"I guess not." We went farther down the hall to my room. "Here's where I hang out," I told Felix. "The room's small, but it has the advantage of being far away from my sister."

"Oh, sisters . . ." Felix made a waving motion. "Such smart mouths."

"Not Martha. She won't talk."

"She won't? Count your blessings," Felix said.

I could see that the two of us were going to get along.

3

B.J.'s Sick Poem

My dad and grandfather were getting ready to go up to northern Minnesota for Christmas trees. Another guy, a friend of Grandpa's who had a big open-bed truck, was driving them. Grandpa and this other man, Everett, sold Christmas trees on a vacant lot every year. Everett's wife, Sally, made wreaths and door hangings out of evergreen and berries and pinecones, and had her own place where she sold them.

"Maybe you could work with Sally, Rachel," Grandma Alice said to Mom as we sat around the breakfast table. "She makes quite a bit of money, and she'd probably be glad to have a real artist helping her."

"Mother," my mom said, shoving oatmeal into Martha's mouth, "I am not exactly that kind of artist. I don't do crafts."

My grandmother raised her eyebrows slightly. "I'm not putting you down, Rachel," she said. "I'm just suggesting it as a convenient way to make money. I always let Sally use the back screened-in porch, so you'd be right here."

"Oh, all right," Mom said. She leaned over to retrieve the spoon that Martha had knocked to the floor. She

DEFIANCE PUBLIC LIBRARY

didn't even bother to rinse it off; nothing made Martha sick. "I guess I might as well bring in money somehow, since I can't get back into my real work right now."

The phone rang, and Grandpa got it. "That was Everett," he said after he hung up. "He'll be here in about twenty minutes."

Mom put a pancake on the tray of Martha's chair and then turned to Dad. "I hope you have a chance to look around," she said, "since you'll be right in our targeted area. See what the houses are like up there. But don't make any commitment until I have a chance to come up and check out the scenery."

That's just like my mother. *Check out the scenery.* Not the schools, not the neighborhood, not the stores, but the *scenery.* Of course, where they wanted to move, there might not be a neighborhood. And the school would probably be so far away that I might as well live in the school bus.

"Kids," my grandmother said, meaning my parents, "I really wonder if you realize what it would mean, living so far from everything like that."

"It would mean living away from chemical waste, radiation, traffic congestion—"

"Rachel," my grandfather interrupted, "we all know your views on the environment, but have you stopped to consider whether you could honestly be happy living up in the north woods?"

This time my dad spoke up. "Artists can be happy anywhere," he said. "As long as they're in touch with their inner selves."

"Well, your daughter," Grandma said, looking at Martha, "is in touch with her pancake."

We all turned toward my sister. She was holding the pancake up to her face. She had already picked out holes for her eyes and mouth.

"What a slob," I muttered.

"It could have been worse," Mom said, struggling with Martha to release her hold on the pancake. "It could have had butter and syrup on it. If I were the kind of mother who allowed cholesterol and sugar in my child's diet."

Martha was just so disgusting. The whole area around her was littered with pieces of toast, globs of cereal she had flung, and now the chunks of pancake she was tearing loose. Cleaning up after a meal with Martha was like mopping up after a massacre.

I was glad to leave for school.

*

It was cold. Kids were standing around in clumps near the doors, waiting for them to open. I spotted Felix and went over.

"Man, it's freezing," I said.

"Not cold enough for the lake to freeze, though. I hope it's solid by the time of the Snowfest."

I hunched deeper into my ski jacket collar. "What's a Snowfest?"

"A big event we have around here in late January. Almost everyone takes part."

"Doing what?" I stamped my feet. Why didn't they open the doors?

"Making snow sculptures. Racing across the lake on

skates or snowmobiles. Sliding down really long ice slides, things like—well, would you look at that!"

I turned to look. Some kid was coming toward us, looking right at Felix.

"B.J.," he said. "My day is ruined." Then he went into a stupid routine of holding up his hands and turning his head sideways and backing away. "Don't come any closer! You're full of disgusting disease!"

Billie Jo stopped about a yard away from Felix. She was wearing a big blue knitted beret, and a glittery scarf in a different shade of blue was wound around her neck. Red wisps of hair stuck out from the beret, and her face was covered with about a zillion freckles.

"What's your problem, Mister Computer?" she asked. "A power outage in the brain department?"

"Oh, B.J., you're just so sick. You were before, and now you're sick in another way, with germs, so stay away."

B.J. turned to stare at me. "Who are you?"

"That's Dan," Felix said before I had a chance. "Keep your distance from him, too. He's my main man."

"I pity you, I really do," B.J. said to me. "Too bad I was out, or I'd have warned you about this mental short circuit."

Just then there was a rush toward the doors that had finally been unlocked. B.J. swooped ahead of us, and I lost her in the crowd.

"How come you guys don't like each other?" I asked Felix.

"Couldn't you *see?* I mean, what a subhuman she is?"

"What I saw mostly was the biggest bunch of freckles

I've ever—" and then I stopped. What a goof! Felix had almost as many, if not more. And red hair, too, the same shade as B.J.'s. They had the same type of looks; that's probably why they didn't get along. "Not that there's anything wrong with freckles," I went on, hoping to smooth over what I'd said before.

"Oh, I know that," Felix said. "It's not her looks, but her personality that's so sickening. Just wait till you know her. You'll see what I mean."

*

Actually, I found out fairly fast.

"Sit down, Dan," the teacher said as I hovered in the front of the room.

"Where shall I sit?"

"Why . . ." The teacher looked up and saw B.J. in the seat. It seemed to me that the teacher's face—before she caught herself—had a look of *Oh no, that's just what I need.* In a regular voice, though, she said I could move to a seat in back.

I liked it there. It gave me a chance to scope out everybody without their knowing it. First I looked at Amanda . . . well, her back. Today she was wearing a fuzzy pink sweater, and there was a pink band holding back her long, very dark, very shiny hair.

I tried to pick out Shirley and Traci, the two girls Felix had said he liked, but couldn't decide who they were.

The teacher called out the names of a couple of kids who were still talking, and when they stopped she said, "We all want to welcome back Billie Jo, who has been ill."

Her smile turned to a frown when several kids made chicken noises.

"That's enough," the teacher said. "Just quiet down. Yes, Billie Jo?" she said, noticing her hand waving in the air.

"I just want to tell the class that I *tremendously* appreciated the many cards and letters and flowers they sent."

The kids looked around at each other, shrugging in a way that said, *I didn't send any, did you?*

"And," Billie Jo went on, standing up, "I have a little poem to read to the class, to show how I feel."

"Billie Jo, that won't be necess—" the teacher began, but B.J. was already striding to the front of the room.

Her red hair, hanging loose now, was snarly looking. She was wearing a skimpy skirt, and over her blouse hung a bright green vest covered with beads and feathers. She had on earrings, too. They were big hoops with glitter on them. I'd seen a lot of far-out jewelry at art fairs, but nothing as tacky as the hoops dangling from B.J.'s ears.

Ignoring the looks the kids were giving her, she cleared her throat and read:

> *"Roses are red, violets are blue.*
> *I had the pox,*
> *And so will you."*

The kids shifted and looked at one another. What was this?

> *"Daisies are white, geraniums are red.*
> *When you break out in spots,*
> *You'll wish you were dead."*

"Thank you very much," the teacher said. "Now—"
"There's more," B.J. told her and went on.

> *"Pansies are purple, sunflowers are yellow.*
> *I'll be eating cheeseburgers*
> *While you're eating Jell-O."*

There were mumblings from the class now.
"Billie Jo," the teacher said, "that's quite enough. You may go sit down."
"Just one more verse," Billie Jo said.

> *"So when you're red and itchy,*
> *All you airheads and jocks,*
> *Just thank your friend B.J.*
> *For giving you the pox."*

She dipped her knee in a fake curtsy, moved the freckles around her face with a smile, and went back to her seat.

The kids began hissing and making comments. A couple of the girls gave little whines and leaned as far away as possible from Billie Jo's seat.

With a sour smile, the teacher said, "Thank you, Billie Jo, for that inspiring message." And to the class, "Can you all quiet down now and get to work?"

One of the girls started waving her hand in the air.

"Yes, Shirley?"

"Are we all really going to . . . to catch chicken pox?" There was a little whimper in her voice. Shirley was one of the girls Felix liked. Looking at her, I couldn't see why.

"Of course you're not going to catch it," the teacher said in a no-nonsense way. "Chicken pox has a contagious period, but that time's long past."

"When was it?" someone blurted out.

The teacher sighed and glanced at the clock. "Right at first, when the person's coming down with it. And even then you'd have to have close contact with the carrier."

"Like kissing?" some kid toward the back called out. Most of the boys looked at B.J. and made gagging sounds. The girls gave little squeals of disgust.

"The subject is closed," the teacher said. "I want it quiet in here!" She walked into one of the aisles, turned a kid's head around for him, and then shot a question about the assignment to someone across the room.

The class settled down, but it seemed like the threat of B.J.'s poem hovered over all of us. I found myself rubbing my forearms against my shirt. What was I doing, rubbing away germs? I doubted they could be gotten rid of that way.

I knew it was weird, but I couldn't help wondering if I'd picked up chicken pox from sitting at B.J.'s desk last week. No. That was impossible.

But what if I had?

I couldn't have. B.J. was long gone by the time I'd sat there. Besides, you could only catch the disease from personal contact. Like kissing.

I glanced in B.J.'s direction. Yuk. What a horrible thought.

4

Lunch with Amanda

At lunch in the cafeteria, Felix was in line right behind me. "Hey, see Shirley and Traci over there at the middle table? Let's sit with them, and you can give me some input on which girl I should zero in on."

"Okay." I wondered what would happen after he zeroed in.

Felix's voice was just above a whisper. "I'd give Shirley two points over Traci for looks, but she's low in the personality rating. Oh, no, would you look at that?"

I looked. B.J. was putting her heaped tray at the end of the girls' table. As we watched, Shirley and Traci moved down a seat. If I'd been B.J., I'd have been hurt and embarrassed. She was acting as if she didn't notice.

"Wouldn't you think B.J. would take the hint and leave?" Felix said.

I had to hand over my plate for lasagna just then, so I didn't answer. It seemed to me the girls were acting like jerks.

After we got our milk, Felix headed for the girls' table and I followed. We sat opposite Shirley and Traci. They didn't seem all that thrilled to see us, either, but maybe they were just putting on an act.

Out of the corner of my eye, I saw someone else heading for our table. I almost hyperventilated when it turned out to be Amanda. *The girl.*

"This place taken?" she asked, pausing at the empty chair between the girls and B.J.

"Help yourself," Traci said, "if you're not fussy about who you sit next to."

"I guess I'm not too fussy," Amanda said, taking her seat. "I'm sitting next to you."

I couldn't help staring across the table at her. Close up she was even more of a knockout. And she was cool, too.

Amanda flipped back her hair and opened her milk carton. She took the paper off her straw and crumpled it. She was probably only the second person I have met in my lifetime who didn't blow the paper at someone opposite. If she'd blown it at me, I'd have saved the paper forever.

"So, guys," B.J. said to all of us, "how did you like my poem?"

"It stunk," Felix said. "It stunk all the way from here to Chicago."

"Yeah, Chicago," Shirley agreed.

"It was a good rhyming poem, B.J.," Amanda said diplomatically. Then she turned to me. "Aren't you from Chicago, Dan?"

She remembered my name! I swallowed a chunk of food and almost choked. "We were there for a while," I said, "but we lived in New Mexico before that."

"I went to Chicago once," Shirley said. That's all. She went to Chicago. Were we supposed to be impressed out of our skulls?

"I've been there three times," Traci said. Was this mind-boggling or what?

"Big deal, you've been out of Wisconsin," B.J. said with a withering look. "Sometimes you guys are so provincial."

"Provincial," Felix explained, "means having a small-town attitude. Hey—there's nothing wrong with that." For the rest of the meal, he talked almost exclusively to Shirley and Traci. Frankly, I couldn't see what he saw in either of them.

*

When I went around to the back of my grandparents' house the next day and in through the screened porch, I saw gobs of greenery heaped onto a big worktable on the porch. There were big sacks, too, that seemed to be loaded with pinecones, and branches with red berries. Dad and Grandpa must have come back.

I went into the house with a feeling of dread. Had my father found a beaten-down old log cabin in the woods somewhere? If so, how soon would we have to move?

He and Mom and Grandpa were sitting at the dining room table, drinking coffee. Dad didn't look as if he was bursting with news, and Mom seemed let down. Hardly daring to hope, I asked about the trip. I didn't come right out and ask about the cabin, though. I guess I had a bit of kid superstition—if you don't talk about something it might not be there. Like monsters.

"Well, we got the trees and everything," Dad said, "but we had car trouble on the way up and that made us lose time. So I didn't have a chance to check out any houses."

"I still think you could have stayed over another night," Mom said. "As long as you were right in the area."

"Honey," Dad said, "it was Everett's truck, and he had to get back." He reached over and patted her hand. "I told you, we'll drive up on our own and look around."

"When?"

"Soon."

Mom looked annoyed.

"Rachel," Grandpa said, "there's no need to rush. Just stay a while. The log cabin isn't going to fall apart that fast."

"Fall apart!" I felt panicky. "Do they just come down like that?"

"No, they don't," Mom said, getting up. "It's just an expression. Dad, I think you could be a little more supportive."

"How am I wrong? For wanting to spend some time with my grandchildren? For telling you to stay as long as you like? Is that wrong? If so, tell me how."

"Oh, you know. It's your attitude." Mom got up and went upstairs.

When she was out of hearing, Grandpa said, "I thought when Rachel was a teenager that some day she'd grow out of all this."

"She's just edgy," Dad said, " because time is slipping by

and she's not producing any new work. I guess she's afraid she'll lose touch with the art world."

I wondered if Grandpa was thinking the same thing I was—that she'd have a very hard time keeping in touch in that frozen wasteland where we seemed to be headed.

*

There was plenty of work for everyone over Thanksgiving. Grandma planned an old-fashioned kind of dinner even though she is a nowadays kind of person in looks and attitude. Grandpa and Dad spent a lot of time over at the Christmas tree lot. Dad also helped Mom and the other woman, Sally, wire the holiday wreaths before they put on the trim.

My job was the lousiest of all—taking care of Martha. She wanted to be out on the porch, scattering pinecones all over the place.

"Dan, can't you make her stay in the house?" Mom asked, snatching a can of spray snow out of Martha's hands.

"She keeps getting away," I said. "You want me to put a leash on her?" Actually, that seemed like a sensible idea to me.

"Play games. Read to her," Mom said.

"She doesn't want me to."

"Then watch TV!"

I got Martha out of there before Mom could realize what she'd just said. I'd heard her line—everyone had—about how awful it is for people to use TV as an electronic babysitter.

The only trouble with Martha was she still tore around during the main action of the show. The only parts that held her attention were the commercials.

*

Felix called at about four o'clock on Thanksgiving afternoon.

"I was wondering if you'd like to come over," he said. "See my stuff, play some games."

"I can't right now," I told him. "We're eating dinner, and I don't know when we'll be finished."

"Dinner? This time of day?"

"Well . . . Thanksgiving dinner is a little different."

"You're having the works? Like a real turkey?"

"Sure." I didn't mention that last year, when Mom cooked, we had a totally vegetarian meal. Even the turkey legs were made of some kind of soybean stuff. "Doesn't your mom cook Thanksgiving dinner?"

"Are you kidding? My mother would freak out at the sight of an uncooked bird. We'll eat at some restaurant, but not today. Both my parents are at work, trying to wind up a big project."

"Oh." I felt sorry for Felix, but he sounded cheery enough. "I'm sorry I can't come over now. How about tomorrow?"

"No problem."

When I got back to the table, Mom asked who'd been on the phone. I told her it was a kid named Felix. "Felix Drake, Mom. You met him the other day.

"Oh . . . he must be Arthur Drake's boy!" she said, remembering. "No wonder he looked familiar." Someone passed the turkey, and my mother, forgetting she's a vegetarian, took a big slice. "Mom," she said to Grandma, "whatever happened with . . . you know?"

I glanced up and caught my grandmother's *I'll-tell-you-later* look.

"What, what?" I asked.

"Watt invented the steam engine," Grandpa said.

Fine. They weren't going to tell me. I hate it when grown-ups leave you wondering like that.

◆ ◆ ◆

5

What's Black
and White All Over?

The day after Thanksgiving Grandma Alice had off from work, so she was doing things around the house. I followed her upstairs, dragging Martha along because she wasn't quite so wild around her grandparents.

In one of the guest rooms, Martha scrambled into a rocker and began rocking hard. All my grandmother had to do was give her a look and say, "Slow down, Martha," and my sister slowed down.

"She really minds you," I said.

"Why shouldn't she?" Grandma Alice said, replacing a stack of towels with fresher ones. I guess they'd been sitting around too long.

"She should mind the rest of us, too, but you can see how she acts."

"It's attitude," Grandma said. "She knows she can get by with things with you-know-who."

"Yeah. Doesn't it seem strange to you, Grandma, that she doesn't t-a-l-k?"

"She will when she feels like it. In the meantime, don't think she doesn't know what's going on."

"C'mon, creep," I told Martha, stopping the movement of the rocker. "Next room."

Grandma went into another empty room with more towels, which she put on a brass towel stand. Each of the guest rooms was furnished in a different way. "I hope you don't mind us following you around," I said.

"Not at all. I'm glad for your company."

"Do you get tired of strangers coming into your house as hotel guests?" I asked her.

"No. If I did, I wouldn't do it anymore. We've met some very interesting people. There are two or three couples that come back every year. We exchange Christmas cards."

"Felix thinks this house is just terrific," I said. I pulled Martha off the bed and straightened out the white chenille spread where she'd rumpled it. "He went wild over everything, even the dining room table."

"That's nice. I'm glad you've found a friend." Grandma ran her fingers along the edge of a table. "I guess this room could use a little dusting."

"No one's coming, are they? In November?"

Grandma smiled. "Actually, no. But, Dan, there's something that makes me keep every room ready, regardless." Her smile grew larger. "Would you say I'm compulsive? That I do things I wouldn't actually have to do?"

I shrugged. "I think it's okay for you to be like that."

As I followed them downstairs—Grandma had hold of Martha's hand now—I wondered if this compulsive thing could be inherited. My mom sure did things she didn't have to do. Like move us all over the country.

The phone started ringing, and Grandma answered it.

"It's for you, Dan," she said. Then she went off to the kitchen with Martha.

"Hey, it's me, Felix. You coming over?"

Boy, I wished I could. "I'm not sure. I'm supposed to baby-sit."

"Baby . . . ? Oh, the biting machine. Couldn't you tie her up or something?"

"Naw. I'd like to, though."

"How long will it be?"

"I'll find out." I put down the phone and went through the kitchen to the back porch. "Mom?" She was standing back, letting the fine spray from a fixative settle on a wreath. "How long are you going to be doing this?"

"For hours. Why?"

"I wanted to go over to Felix's house."

"Oh, Dan, I'm sorry, but I can't keep Martha out here, with all this stuff. . . ."

"Okay," I sighed.

Grandma noticed me dragging through the kitchen. "What's up?"

"Nothing. I just have to watch Martha forever. And Felix wanted me to come over."

"Oh, for heaven's sake, go. I'll take care of her. You need to be around kids while you can."

"Thanks!" I picked up the phone and told Felix I'd be right over. He gave directions. I ran and got my jacket and headed out the door. But then Grandma's words came back and made me feel a little less joyful. *Be around kids while you can.* There probably wouldn't be any where we were headed. Not for miles. I'd be like a hermit, holed up with two artists. And an annoying little sister, who was worse than no one at all.

.

Felix's house was several blocks away in an area where all the houses looked new. His was low and flat, with lots of glass. The kitchen, I saw when Felix let me in, was black and white, with everything glassy and shiny. The floor tiles were black, and I noticed they just kept on being black as I followed Felix into the next room.

"I'm really glad you could come over," he said. "It's going to be a long weekend."

"Are your folks around?" The place seemed so quiet and empty.

"No, they both had to go in to work."

"Downtown?"

"Yeah. Chicago."

"Your parents work in *Chicago?*"

"Sure. That's where their offices are. Want to see the rest of the house?"

"Okay." The living room looked really cool, but *cold.* I mean, the black leather sofas weren't the squashy kind that you sink into, but were built on straight lines. The chairs were also leather, with chrome trim. There was just one rug over the black tile floor and it was white and deep and fluffy . . . something to look at rather than to step on.

There were no curtains at the windows, just white blinds. The only color in the room came from some big green plants (in white holders) and a couple of paintings that had a touch of red in otherwise black-and-white designs.

"Who paints, your mother or your father?" I asked Felix.

He stared at me. "What?"

And then I realized that all parents weren't painters themselves. "I meant," I said, fibbing a little, "who goes out and buys the artwork?"

Felix furrowed his brow. "Actually, I think the decorator must have picked these paintings out. I just never thought about it. Want to see the office?"

"Sure."

We stepped into a room next to the living room. It had a continuous counter running around three sides (white, of course) and bookshelves—all the stuff you'd see in a place where people worked. At the two ends of the counter were two computers.

"How come you have two of those?" I asked.

"Well, there's one for each parent," he said, as though it was the most natural thing in the world. "They have their own work, and data, and have to be able to access at any given time."

"Oh, right," I said, again as though I totally understood.

"I'll show you my room, and then we can have a snack," Felix said. We passed a closed door. "Parents' room," he said. We went farther down the hall and into his room. "Here's where I hang out."

Felix's room had posters and rockets like you see in most kids' rooms. But he did have one fairly unusual thing for a boy his age—a personal computer.

"Want to play a game?" he asked. "We might as well start off with the classic game of Adventure."

"Sure," I said. "But I'm a little rusty." *Rusty? Ignorant was more like it.*

"I'll explain as we go along," Felix said. He did, in a way I could understand, and it was fun.

We'd been playing for about an hour when the phone rang. Felix had his own private phone and line.

"Hi, Sheila," he said. "What's up?" He talked on, while I tried playing the game from both angles. I paid no attention to what he was saying, but when he hung up I asked if Sheila was another of his girlfriends.

"Huh? Sheila's my mom."

I felt like a fool.

"She called to say she's going to be late, so I'm supposed to phone the restaurant and make our reservation for later on tonight."

Felix was probably disappointed. His face looked flushed as he called and changed the time.

"Let's go get something to eat," he said. "Or I could order in a pizza or something."

"I'm not that hungry. But go ahead, if you want to. . . ."

"I'm not that hungry, either. I'll make some popcorn."

In the kitchen he took out a package, tore off the wrappings, and stuck it in the microwave. The kitchen looked like a showroom that never got used.

I was going to ask Felix if his mother or father ever cooked, but instead I asked him what they did.

"Sheila's a lawyer with an investment firm," he said, "and Arthur's a broker. He deals in futures."

"Futures?"

"Yeah, like soybeans and pork bellies." Felix took out the puffed-out bag when the oven beeped, got out two bowls (black), and poured in the popcorn. He opened the refrigerator (black) and looked inside. *There was nothing there to eat!* All I could see were some bottles of wine, a whole bunch of different kinds of soda, and what looked like a couple of jars of makeup. Toward the back was a package of imported coffee beans.

I told Felix what kind of soda I wanted, and we took the cans and the popcorn to his room.

As we walked along, I noticed another small bedroom. There was a lot of stuff inside, like books and things on shelves, but I just got a glimpse of them.

"Do you have a brother or sister?" I asked as we went on by.

Felix mumbled, "No one else lives here," which I thought a rather strange answer. But I didn't press him about it.

We ate the popcorn and finished the game, and then we just lolled around, talking. It seemed to me that as time went on, Felix wasn't quite with it.

Finally I said, "Is something wrong?"

He brushed his sleeve across his face. He was looking flushed again, more than before. "To tell you the truth, I don't feel so well."

"Oh. Maybe I'd better leave."

"Maybe you'd better." Felix sounded apologetic. "I should probably lie down for a while. I feel a little weak."

It went through my mind that he could be suffering from malnutrition, considering that there was nothing to eat in the house. "Should I order a pizza or fried chicken or something?"

Felix made an *urp*ing sound, like someone about to throw up. "No, no food. I must be coming down with a virus, like my mom had last week."

"That's too bad."

"Yeah, I'll probably have to miss Thanksgiving dinner with Sheila and Arthur after all."

He looked so down. I wondered if his folks really would go off to dinner and leave him with nothing. I hoped they at least had some canned soup for him in the house.

Felix led the way to the kitchen and patted my shoulder as I was about to leave. "Thanks, pal, for coming over. Sorry to conk out on you like this."

"That's okay. I just wish—"

"What?"

I wanted to say, *that you could come home with me and have Grandma look after you.* Instead, I said, "I wish you didn't have to be sick during vacation."

"I'll be all right in a day or two," he said.

But whenever I called over the weekend, his answering machine said to leave a message. Felix never called back. I hoped the so-called virus hadn't turned into something serious. Or that Felix hadn't decided he didn't want to be my friend after all.

6

What's Red and Spotty All Over?

Wen I walked into the classroom Monday morning, the kids were buzzing around more than usual. I asked someone what was going on.

"You haven't heard?" He laughed. "Felix has chicken pox!"

Oh, no. *And I'd been with him when he was first coming down with them.* I felt my forehead. Didn't it seem somewhat feverish? I asked Mom a week or two ago if I'd ever had chicken pox, and she said no. Now maybe I did have it, or was about to.

I noticed B.J. smarting off to kids around her. She was saying in a loud voice that the whole room was probably infected, just as she'd predicted in her poem.

The teacher came into the room just then. "I suppose you've all heard the news," she said. "Felix has chicken pox. Now don't get into a panic. It isn't likely any of you will get it unless you've been in close contact with him."

Great, I thought. I'd been pretty close to Felix. But then I wondered how he could have gotten the pox from

B.J. He'd made it pretty clear that he thought she was some kind of lowlife he couldn't stand to be around.

At lunchtime I really wanted to sit next to Amanda, but I didn't have the courage. Besides, if I was coming down with chicken pox, I'd never forgive myself if Amanda caught it from me. Sitting there by myself, I felt so alone. I didn't really belong here, in this school. In another month I could be history. I might never see Amanda again.

.

I was cutting through the lot after school when B.J. came along and started walking with me, just as though we were old buddies. I was really surprised.

"You going over to see Felix?" she asked.

"No. Well, I'd like to, but—"

She dismissed my words with a wave. "If you're gonna get the pox, you've already got it." She pulled a candy bar out of her pocket. It was smushed up, and some strings of gum were stuck to the wrapper. "Those vile, loathsome germs are cruising through your blood, getting ready for a touchdown landing."

My skin began to itch.

B.J. took a bite of the chocolate bar. The melted stuff from the wrapper left smears around her mouth. "Oh, excuse me." She held the candy toward me. "Want a bite?"

"No, thanks." The bar looked revolting. I wondered how much time it had served in her pocket.

"Don't be scared. You can't catch anything from me

now." She wiped her chocolatey mouth with the end of her scarf.

"Really, I don't want any." I had the feeling she knew I'd been at Felix's over the weekend. But how could she know?

Finally B.J. finished the bar, licked off the rest of the chocolate from the wrapper, crumpled the paper, and stuck it into her pocket. At least she wasn't a litterer. Mom would like that about B.J., if nothing else.

We walked on a ways. I wondered when she was going to leave.

"So," she said after a bit, "you want me to come over to your house?"

What could I say? *Actually, no. Of course not.* "Okay," is what I said. What a spineless blob I was.

"What's there to do?" B.J. asked. Now she was making like I was some kind of entertainment committee.

"There's nothing to do," I said. Maybe she'd change her mind.

She took off her crazy big knitted beret and spun it around on a finger. "Don't worry about it," she said. "I can usually improvise."

Meaning what, I wondered.

"Don't you know any girls?" I asked, hoping she'd take the hint and go somewhere else.

"Of course I know girls. If you haven't noticed, half the kids in our class are girls." She was now spinning the beret crazily. "They're such airheads. Not one of them has any ambition."

I thought about Amanda. Surely she wasn't an airhead. "What do you mean," I asked, "no ambition? To do what?"

"To go places."

"What places?"

She gave me her now-familiar rolling-of-the-eyes routine. "When I say 'places,' I don't mean 'places.' Ambition. Drive. The old pizzazz. *You* know."

I didn't, but I didn't want her to know I didn't. "Oh, yes, that," I said.

"I already know what I'm going to be," B.J. said. "An artist."

"Why would you want to be an artist?" I asked. It was the last thing *I'd* choose to be.

"Why? So I'll be rich and famous and can do anything I want. People will knock themselves out just to get close to me. Kids'll brag that they knew me back when." Her face was pink and excited. She looked as though she was hopping on springs. It was too bad she was due for such a disappointment.

"I hate to tell you this," I said, "but most artists aren't all that rich and famous."

"I'm not most artists. I'm a talent. I was born with it, like Bette Midler and Madonna."

B.J. was so stupid! "Those people aren't artists," I told her.

"Who says?"

"They don't draw or paint. Or if they do, that's not what they're famous for."

She just stared at me.

"Look. My parents are good at it, but people don't stop them for autographs."

B.J. stared at me some more. "They're good at *what?*"

"Drawing, painting."

"So?"

"So you said you were going to be a painter and be rich and famous."

"I did not say I was going to be a painter. I said I was going to be an artist. Don't you get it? Artist with a capital A. An *entertainer,* you idiot."

"Oh." I did feel like an idiot. It's just that I'd met so many of the regular artist-artists in my life.

I didn't want to be around this irritating girl any longer. "B.J.," I said, "I just remembered. I have to do something when I get home."

I was trying frantically to think of a lie I could tell her when she asked me what. But she didn't ask. She just gave a little nod, turned, and went off in the opposite direction. It was almost as though she expected to be sent away, as though it happened all the time.

And now that I saw her going off like a dog that's used to being yelled at, I felt bad about telling her the lie. Would it have hurt me to be a little friendly? Who was I to be fussy, anyway?

Then, as I watched, B.J. started doing some crazy kind of dance, snapping her fingers and wriggling her skinny hips. She didn't look a bit let down, at least not from the back. I'll bet she was singing, too, and rolling her eyes, acting like she was some big-deal entertainer.

What a nut. I'd done right to tell her I had something

to do at home. It wasn't an actual lie, anyway. I could always count on taking care of Martha, who was a nuisance but at least didn't talk crazy. Maybe she would, though, if the day ever came when she did talk. With that awful thought, I turned and headed for home.

7

First and Last Snow Fight

M y father was sitting at the kitchen table working on some papers when I came into the house. He was wearing his Swedish deer-patterned turtleneck and cords.

"Hi, Dad, were you substitute teaching today?" I asked.

He looked up and gave his slow smile. "How could you tell?"

"You're wearing your good clothes, including the heartbreak sweater." That's what Mom called it, because it brought out the intense blue of Dad's eyes.

"Yeah, I always give my students a break the first day," Dad said, going along with the gag. "I'm supposed to fill in two days for this teacher, maybe even more. From now on they'll see me in my old paint-smeared grubbies."

A hope rose in me. Maybe Dad was beginning to dig in here. He might get used to the place and want to stay.

"Are you making lesson plans for . . . for the next few weeks?" I asked. That's what it looked like.

"Oh, no." He picked up his pencil again. "For this class

I'm just continuing what they've already started. What I'm doing now is jotting down some new ideas I'd like to try myself sometime. I may do them when we move."

So much for hope. "Did anyone call?" I went over and hung my coat on the hook.

"Yes. The number's there on the counter."

It was Felix, of course. Who else would call me?

"What did they say about me at school?" Felix wanted to know.

"Not much. Some kids went down to the office."

"Because they thought they were getting chicken pox?"

"Could be. But I'd guess they just wanted to get out of class."

"Seems reasonable. How do you feel? Any fever, spots?" Felix sounded almost hopeful.

"No."

"Oh." Now he sounded almost let down. "I was think-ing if we had chicken pox at the same time we could hang out together."

This seemed to me like a high price to pay for friend-ship, but then I'm not into suffering.

"You're not there all alone, are you?" I asked.

"Sure. But my parents call once or twice a day." And as though he sensed my slight shock he added, "I'm okay, Dan, only I get tired doing my computer thing. It would be fun if you were here." His voice got squeaky.

"You okay?"

"Yeah, but my eyes are beginning to water. I'd better sign off."

"Right. Better get some rest now." That sounded so par-entish, I added, "Drink your banana juice, wear your boots to bed, and rest your eyes by watching at least ten movies every day."

"Yes, doctor. Try to come over Saturday," Felix practi-cally wheezed. "Promise?"

"Sure." I wondered what kind of computer thing he was doing. I'd be no help, but at least I could keep him com-pany.

*

The Christmas trees over at the lot were selling pretty well. It was still early for people to put them up, but some families bought while there was such a good selection and just let the trees sit in buckets of water outside their houses.

The big sellers were the wreaths and sprays that Mom helped make. They were the kinds of things people put on their front doors to show they were getting into the holi-day spirit.

"I saw Sally this evening at the grocery store," Grandma said to Mom at the dinner table one night, "and she's thrilled with the way those things are selling. She even upped the prices this year because they're so much more artistic than they ever were before."

You'd think that would please my mother, but oh, no.

"They're ticky-tacky craft things, not art," Mom said. She wiped some crud off Martha's chin.

"I see no need to brand them *ticky-tacky*," Grandma

said. "For what they are, they're very well done, thanks to you."

"For what they are is right," Mom said. "Oh, Martha! You are just such a pain sometimes!" *Pain* was pretty mild for what my sister had just done—scooped up all the whole wheat bread pudding from her plate and heaved it overboard.

It snowed on Thursday, the first snow of the season. The kids at school seemed happy beyond belief. I couldn't understand why. It wasn't a snow day, with no school. There was no blizzard. Just a couple of inches lying on the ground when we woke up and then a little more off and on during the day.

At lunch hour, I had no one to eat with so I sat alone. If I'd thought we were going to stay here for a year or two, I'd have made an effort to get some more friendships going. But what was the point? Finally, because there was plenty of room at my table, some guys sat down. They didn't even say hi.

I shut my mind to their talk, but little by little I couldn't help but hear what they were saying. Something about getting out early.

". . . Forts like last year," I heard a kid named Joe say. "We'll pulverize them."

"Who?" someone asked.

"Those baby fifth-graders. If they're not too chicken to fight."

"We weren't last year," Joe said.

"I know, but we weren't babies, either."

I wondered how these guys got off calling kids just a year younger *babies*. Of course, I didn't know what they were talking about, either.

Just then B.J. wandered over. The guys held up their hands to shield their faces and leaned sideways away from her. "Get away, germ ball!"

"Shut up, Joe," B.J. said, sitting down. "Or I'll kiss you on the mouth."

This really raised a racket. The teacher supervisor stood up and pinned his look on our group.

"So . . . ," B.J. said directly to me, "did they have this custom at the last school you went to?"

I felt on the spot. Quietly, I said, "You mean, kissing on the mouth?"

The guys whooped and laughed so loudly, the teacher took a few steps in our direction. I felt myself blushing. I wanted to dissolve and disappear.

B.J. laughed, too. Today her bushy red hair had one bunch of it pulled up and fastened with a big band of zebra-striped leather. A jungly-looking necklace with glittery animals hanging from it circled her neck. "Hey, maybe we'll start a kissing custom, huh, Joe?" She gave a little wriggle. "I'll bet you'd like that, as long as you were customized with Kelsey."

"Beat it," Joe muttered. His face had turned pink, and he avoided looking at his laughing friends.

"No one would ever kiss *you*, B.J.," one of them said.

"Oh, Troy," she said sweetly, "I wouldn't deign to bestow my affection on any of you slime bags, anyway. I have more class than to do anything that disgusting."

By now the teacher supervisor was fairly close to us. Not saying anything, just letting everyone know he was ready to pounce.

His presence gave me a little courage. "Uh . . . what kind of forts were you talking about?" I asked Troy.

He glanced up, met the teacher's gaze, and turned to me, saying, "It's a tradition here. The first snow of the year that falls on a school day, we get out early to make forts or whatever."

I'd never heard of such a thing. "How come?"

He shrugged. "Don't ask me. We've just always done it."

"I hear some of the girls are going to build a snow woman," B.J. said. She reached for one of Joe's fries. Joe, looking annoyed, shoved the whole tray in front of her. She acted pleased, as though Joe was being nice instead of insulting.

"There's no such thing as a snow *woman*, B.J.," a kid down the line said. "I've never seen one."

"Which proves nothing," Billie Jo said. "You haven't seen a shark, either, so does that mean there aren't any?" Her eyes met mine. "Do you believe these clods?"

I wished she wouldn't do this to me. I didn't want to side with her (although she was right) and get on the bad side of all the guys.

At that moment the bell rang. Saved.

What I found really hard to believe was that we actually were getting out early . . . *to play in the snow.* But we were. The announcement came over the loudspeaker saying we'd be let out an hour and a half early and that everyone was expected to participate in some way.

*

There seemed to be two teams building snow forts. They rolled up the biggest balls they could, joined them together with more snow, and curved them just a little on each end, for protection. Some of the kids were making snowball ammunition and piling it up behind the barricades.

Because Joe and Troy had been halfway friendly at lunch, I joined their group. They didn't go overboard welcoming me or anything, but on the other hand, they didn't tell me to leave. The fort itself was almost finished. I started making snowballs for the fight, which would start pretty soon, I guessed.

Some of the girls were a little way off, building their snowmen, or snow women, or whatever they were. But a few girls were helping at the forts.

"Now listen, you babes," a kid named Sheldon said, "when the fight starts, you sit down here, behind the wall, and hand us the snowballs."

"In the first place," B.J. piped up, "where do you get off, calling us *babes?* And in the second place, don't expect us to serve up the snowballs. This is our fight, too."

"Oh, B.J., why don't you just shut that big mouth of yours?"

She stood with her hands on her hips, her chin in the air. "Why don't you make me? I'm not a *babe* but you're a *baby.*"

Sheldon leaped at her. She sidestepped, and he crashed into the fort, knocking off part of the top. Then B.J. lit out, with Sheldon chasing after her. They zigzagged around the lot. Finally, he caught hold of her scarf, then got a grip on her, flung her to the ground, and pushed her face into the snow.

A lot of the kids were watching and yelling, mostly for Sheldon.

It worried me. "Couldn't she suffocate or something?" I said to some kid.

"Naw, she's tough. She can take care of herself."

I wasn't so sure about that. I ran over and saw that B.J. was really pinned down. She couldn't move her shoulders and arms, and her face was really in the snow.

I yanked at Sheldon and pulled him away. "Leave her alone!" I yelled. "You're crazy, you want to kill her?"

He looked confused, sprawled there in the snow.

Billie Jo turned her face toward me. It was wet and white-looking, and the freckles stood out like a join-the-dots puzzle. She stood up then, brushed herself off, and said to Sheldon, "I was about to throw you, you know that."

"Sure you were." He looked at me. "Why don't you just butt out, New Boy?"

The other guys added a few comments and then followed Sheldon back to the fort.

B.J. wiped her face with the end of her scarf. "You didn't have to do that," she said to me. "I can take care of myself."

I stared at her. "You're welcome."

She stared back and blinked. "Oh . . . well . . . thanks."

I gave a little nod and turned to walk away. But where

to? I'd probably be kicked right out of the fort. No one wanted a new kid around, especially one who'd just run off to rescue a girl like Billie Jo.

I leaned against a tree, feeling miserable and alone. Was I always going to be an outsider?

◆ ◆ ◆ ───────────────────

8

A Super Snow Woman

It had started snowing again, and the fight was going strong. B.J. ran out from the fort opposite Sheldon's, carrying a bunch of balls in a scarf she'd fixed up like a sling.

B. J. sure had guts. Even taking a few hits didn't seem to faze her. I was trying to get up the nerve to join her team when someone behind me asked if I could help them.

I turned and saw Amanda. She looked prettier than ever with her cheeks turned rosy, and specks of snow glittering in her dark hair. Was she really talking to *me?*

"Help with what?" I asked, trying to keep my voice steady. And thinking, *Anything, anything, just say the word.*

"We can't lift part of our snow woman, and it would get too big if we rolled it anymore." She smiled. "Could you carry it for us?"

I shrugged, not trusting my voice. And smiled. And followed her.

We got to a place where a girl, Heidi somebody, stood beside a pretty big snowball. "Could you lift it and carry it over there?" Amanda asked, pointing.

"Sure." *Don't let me stumble, don't let me drop it.*

I got the ball to the spot Amanda indicated and stuck it on top of a big base made of packed snow. In the meantime, someone had rolled a ball for the head. Heidi put it in place.

"You're making a snow *woman*, huh?" I asked. "What do you do next, to make it . . . you know . . . womanlike?"

"I guess fill it in to make a skirt, and I don't know . . . arms?" Heidi asked.

"It would be nice to give it long hair, too," I said.

"Oh, right!" Amanda turned to Heidi. "If you'll fix the skirt, I'll do the arms. . . . How would I do the arms?" she asked me.

Suddenly I, who had mostly lived in warm places, and who hadn't made a snowman in years, was the expert here.

"Just slap up a bunch of snow against the main part and then carve arms out of it."

"Oh." Amanda said. "Right. That's what I'll do." She made a little frown.

"Want me to help?" I offered.

The frown changed into a smile. "Oh! Would you?"

Of course I would.

The arms weren't hard to do, because we had them close to the body and not sticking out. "How about the hair?" I asked, getting into it.

"Would you help us with that, too?" Amanda was really involved in this.

"Sure."

We packed some snow around the head. By this time

the girls were just watching, as though I was in charge. I looked around at the forts. The snowball fight was still going on, but no one seemed to need me, or miss me, or anything. Well . . . why should they?

When the snow for the hair was in place, I tried to model it with my fingers. It didn't look bad, but it could be better. I needed a sculptor's tool.

"Do any of you have a comb?" I asked. One girl held out a little one. "No, that's too fine. I'd like to have . . ."

"A pick?" Heidi turned and said, "Gloria, you have one, don't you?"

The girl named Gloria zipped open a little bag fastened to her belt and produced just the kind of comb I needed— wide, with sharp, spaced teeth. I didn't know they were called picks.

I made the hair long and wavy, with bangs.

"How about the face?" someone asked. "Should we find pebbles or something for the eyes?"

"Not good enough for our snow woman," I said. Where did I get that *our?*

"What'll we do, then?" Heidi asked.

"We'll sculpt the features, like on a real statue." I looked at the group of girls. They were standing there, waiting for me. Me . . . the big expert! I'd never done anything like this before, but this was no time to back away.

"I'll need something to carve with. . . ."

The girls rummaged around in their pockets for anything that might work. I collected a pencil stub, a small mirror, and a six-inch flexible ruler to shape and smooth the features. They worked pretty well. In a few minutes, I'd actually created a face.

I took a few steps backward to get the whole view and stepped on someone's toes.

"Sorry," I said and turned. It was Troy! Then I saw a whole ring of guys standing there. How long had they been watching?

Great. Now I'd be labeled a sissy who hung around girls all the time.

The guys went over to the snow woman and walked around her. I hoped none of them would do something stupid, like knock off her head. If he did, then I'd have to take him on in a fight, to save face in front of Amanda. I might have to take on *several*, in fact, and totally lose my face as it looked now.

"Hey, Wakefield," one of the guys said, "how come you did that?"

"Because I asked him to!" Amanda said, with a touch of defiance.

"Ohhh . . . he did it for you!" It was Joe, acting big. "He made this fancy statue for Amanda! Wooooo!"

"Oh, shut up," Amanda said. "You think you're so cool."

"Well, I am cool. In fact, I'm freezing. How about you, Wakefield, are you cool? Or do you think you're hot?" Joe's laugh was actually a *hah, hah, hah*, like you see in comic strips.

"I'm hot enough to take you on . . ." I wanted to use his last name, too, but I didn't know it, so I just substituted *jerk*.

"Ooooooh! He wants to take me on! What do you think, guys?"

"Do it!" It sounded unanimous.

Joe stomped toward me, paying no attention to yells from the girls. Amanda tried to come between us, but he shoved her aside. Now I was really riled. No matter what happened, I had to fight.

Without even thinking, I lowered my head and butted Joe in the stomach. With a grunt, he fell backward. I wasn't quick enough, though. He rose, grabbed my ankles, and sent me sprawling. Then we were all over each other, hitting some, but mostly just trying to subdue each other there in the snow. I don't know how long the fight went on, but suddenly I was face down in the snow the way B.J. had been earlier. I couldn't raise my head. I couldn't breathe.

Suddenly my head was jerked up by the hair. Freedom! Air! I took it in in huge gulps. Was it a teacher who'd saved me? One of the guys? No. It was Billie Jo. Great. Rescued by a *girl!*

She was yelling at the guys now, telling them off. It seems there'd been three guys holding me down.

"He shouldn't have called Joe a jerk," one of them alibied.

"You're right," B.J. said. "He should have called him a cowardly, sick-headed scuzz. Like all of you are."

I don't know what would have happened next, because just then the principal appeared. Where was he when I needed him?

"What's going on here?" the principal asked.

"Uh . . . ," Troy said. "We just came over to see what the girls . . . and Dan, here, were doing."

"I see." The principal looked as though he knew it was more than that, but hey, it had been a long day. And there was no show of blood. "All right," he said. "I just want to remind you that fighting is not on the approved list of activities here at school . . . and after today that includes snowball fighting. Understood?"

The kids gave little grunts.

The principal nodded and went on. "The dismissal bell is about to ring. If there's anything you need inside, get it now. Otherwise, wait in line for the bus."

The kids drifted away. Amanda stood there, though, staring at the snow woman. "I wish I didn't have to leave her," she said. "She probably won't be here tomorrow."

"It may stay cold enough," I said.

"But someone will knock her over, trample on her. I know they will," Amanda said. "Some of these kids are so vicious."

"You can always make another."

"It won't be the same."

"I guess not. Once I heard my dad say if you copy a work of art, it isn't the same . . . it loses its spark." Then I realized how stupid that sounded. "Don't get me wrong. I'm not saying the snow woman is a work of art."

"But she is, in her own way." Amanda's face glowed as she looked at it. "I think our snow sculpture is wonderful." Her look shifted to me, and she was still glowing. "You have such natural talent, Dan. You're so lucky."

Just then someone called her name. "Amanda, your bus is loading."

She dashed away, but at the top step of the bus she turned to wave.

I smiled and waved back. My feeling of loneliness was gone, at least for now.

9

Dan's Winter Dream

I expected Mom to quiz me about my wet hair when I got home, but she didn't even notice. She was sitting at the kitchen table with Dad, drinking herbal tea.

"What's up?" I asked.

"Nothing." But she kept on talking to Dad about this woman she'd met downtown, an old high school friend, and how boring her life sounded. "Can you believe she's never been out of this place? Except for a honeymoon trip to who knows where and a visit to some relatives in Missouri."

"Maybe she likes it here," I said.

Mom gave me a glance, as though to say *No one's talking to you,* but then she went on. "And I couldn't believe it when Maggie said, 'I have a picture of you stuck in our high school yearbook, from the newspaper, when you won a big art award.'"

"Well, that's nice," Dad said. "Local girl makes good."

Mom sighed. "But what have I done lately? I haven't had a brush in my hand for weeks."

A silence followed, and before Mom could start up

again, I said, "They let us out early today, to have snow fights."

"They *what?*" Dad shifted his gaze to stare at me.

"Yeah, they did. Look at my hair." I ruffled it to show them how wet it was.

"The school let you do it?" Dad asked. "That's unusual."

"It's a tradition in this town," Mom said. "Go dry off your hair, Dan. And don't wake up Martha when you go upstairs."

*

Felix called me after dinner. "Just my luck to miss the big snow fight," he said. "Was it a blast?"

"Yeah." I decided I might as well confess; he'd probably find out anyway. "I didn't really take part in the fight. I had to help . . ."

"She told me about it. She said you're really an artist."

I felt a pang of jealousy. Was Amanda so close to Felix that she'd call him? "Listen, it was no big deal. Just a snow woman."

"Another thing she said was that you may be a twerpy new kid but . . ."

Amanda called me a twerpy new kid? I felt really deflated.

". . . You showed some real spunk in saving her from the sleaze pack."

"Felix—" Now I was confused. "Who are we talking about?"

"Billie Jo . . . who else?"

Billie Jo. Whew. What a relief.

"So try to come over on Saturday unless you get chicken pox in the meantime. Has anyone else gotten it? Say yes."

"Not that I know of. So far it's just you and B.J." A thought occurred to me. "Isn't it funny that you two are the only ones who got the pox and you have the same . . . well, the same kind of looks?" I meant the red hair and freckles, of course.

"It's not so strange when you know the facts," Felix said.

"Right." I figured it must be some genetic thing that smart kids like Felix knew about. And it made me realize again how much I'd missed out on by being shuffled from one school to another. If I could just hang around Felix long enough, I was sure I'd pick up a lot of scientific facts that could come in handy someday.

*

I woke up during the night. The moon was shining right across my bed, like a golden path. I got up and went to the window, meaning to pull down the shade, but instead I stared at the backyard. It was as though some magic hand had tossed diamonds everywhere on the pure white snow. It glittered everywhere except where the trees and the shed laid shadows.

I wondered if Lake Lorraine was frozen, and if so, how it looked in the intense moonlight. And then I thought of the snow woman, standing in the schoolyard. Was she glittering now, too? If we'd made a crown for her head, would it be covered with moon diamonds?

And then I remembered the dream I'd just had. There had been a room . . . a huge room with walls made of snow. And I knew I had to paint pictures on all those walls. I wouldn't be allowed to leave until I'd done it. But I couldn't. Or rather, I wouldn't.

Stupid dream. I turned from the window and went back to bed. What put a dream like that in my mind? I lay there thinking about my day. Amanda . . . what she'd said! *You have such a natural talent, Dan. You're so lucky.* And then B.J. had told Felix over the phone that I was an artist.

I punched down the pillow and flopped over to my side. I wasn't going to be an artist. Artists didn't lead regular lives or let their kids live regular lives. I was going to be something real, something solid. Maybe an overland truck driver, or a scientist who makes some mind-blowing discovery, or a deep-sea diver who explores shipwrecks miles down in the ocean. Maybe I could even learn to do something connected with computers.

Felix was the lucky one. He already knew a lot about computers and had ideas for his future. I wondered if I could learn from him. I knew he'd be willing to give it a try. This was a pleasant thought, and I almost drifted to sleep. But the next thought came like a jolt. *What good does it do to make plans? Your days in this town are numbered, Dan, and you know it. So give it up.*

I didn't sleep well for the rest of the night.

*

The next day at school, Amanda came up to me when we were changing classes. "Did you see what happened to the snow woman?"

"Yeah, some jerks smashed it."

"I felt sad at first," she said, walking along beside me. I noticed she was wearing the pink sweater and hair ribbon again. "But in a way, it's better to have it all gone than to see it slowly melt away. What do you think?"

"Sure." But I was really thinking about what Mom had said once, about how light reflects color. I was noticing the pinkish glow on Amanda's face and wondering if that look could ever be captured by a painter. Hey! Why was I thinking *that?* Who cared?

I wanted to change the subject from the snow woman to let Amanda know I was someone interesting, someone with lots of things to talk about. All I could come up with, though, was Felix's chicken pox and B.J.'s freakish behavior. By then we were at the classroom door, so I was saved from having to say anything at all.

10

Phone Call from Amanda

There was a new development at home. Mom had actually taken up painting again. That was no big breakthrough in my life, except that it gave me hope—a minuscule amount—that she might get so caught up in her art that she'd forget about moving.

Not forever, of course. Let's be realistic. My mother is never one to give up on her plans. Dad likes to say he didn't have a chance, once she made up her mind to marry him. He's kidding, of course, but I suspect it's close to the truth.

Anyway, I was all for encouraging Mom to keep on painting and maybe putting off leaving. With time, anything could happen.

After school I wandered into the bedroom she was using as her studio. She'd pushed the furniture to one side to make more room. "How you doin', Mom?"

She looked at me over the top of her glasses. "I'm trying to rearrange nature." She glanced at her easel and then back at me. "Come here. Tell me what you think."

Mom stood, staring at her watercolor, arms folded, brush in hand.

I went over and took a close look. "It's the backyard, isn't it? Only you moved the tree."

"Ummm." She put down the brush. "Artist's privilege. This way it's a better composition, don't you think?"

"Yeah, I guess." Actually the tree out in the yard looked okay to me where it was. "I'm glad to see you've started to paint again."

"Yes," she said absently. "I need to pile up some work so I can sell it to tourists next summer up north."

Oh, so that was why. I wandered back to my room feeling a little depressed.

When I went downstairs a while later, I saw Grandma had come home. She asked if Dad was around, and just then he walked in the back door.

"Michael, I have some very interesting news," Grandma said.

"Oh?" Dad smiled. "They've made you coach of the basketball team as well as superintendent?"

"They did that a long time ago," Grandma said in the same light tone. "No, what I heard today was that Jeff Noland is leaving his job—for health reasons."

Dad frowned. "Jeff . . . ?"

"The art instructor over at Carter College. You've met him."

"Right." Dad touched the coffee pot to see if it was hot, and reached for a coffee mug. "What does his leaving have to do with me?"

Grandma hesitated, then said, "You could apply for the job."

Dad glanced at her and then away. He poured the coffee. "You know how Rachel has her heart set on going up north."

"And what about you? What do *you* really want?" Grandma asked.

My dad looked undecided for just a moment and then said, "I want whatever makes my wife happy."

I was hoping Grandma would put an arm around my shoulder and say, "What about this kid here? Don't you want to take a shot at making him happy?"

She didn't, though. Dad and she started talking about other things, and then Martha toddled into the room from her late nap.

I wondered what kind of stand my sister would take when she was older and finally decided to talk. Would she yell and carry on about moving, and be so obnoxious my parents would finally give in and say, *Okay, Martha, we'll stay?* I could see that happening. But then I could also see my sister yelling at me, saying I was a wimp for wanting to lead an average kind of life.

I guessed from Mom's lighthearted attitude at dinner that neither Dad nor Grandma had told her about the long-term teaching job Dad could get. Well, why should they? She'd just put down the idea.

"You're cheerful tonight, Rachel," Grandpa said.

"Oh, Dad, I always am when my painting is going well," Mom answered.

"That reminds me," he went on. "I've cleared a part of the attic. We can take the furniture from the room you're using and put it up there so you'll have more space."

Mom patted Grandpa's hand and said he was sweet, but it wasn't worth the effort. "We'll be leaving soon."

"How soon?" I asked, with a catch in my voice.

"As soon as we find the right place." Mom turned to my dad. "Honey, do you think we might take a trip up north next week? Come on," she coaxed, "could we?" In imitation of a little girl having her photo taken, she folded her hands under her chin and gave my father a beseeching look. "Please?"

We all had to smile. Mom could be cute and funny and flirty when she wanted to be. Sometimes, when she got going, she broke Dad and me up. Now, though, I didn't like what she was being flirty about.

"Honey," Grandpa said, "why don't you just relax, enjoy Christmas here? This isn't the time to go on the prowl. Stick around, make it a real family holiday."

I held my breath.

There was a pause, then Mom said, "You're right, Dad. I guess it won't matter if we put the trip on hold for the time being."

I started breathing again. *Reprieved,* at least for now.

Each day we delayed gave me a little more hope. You just never knew what might happen.

*

I almost expected to wake up with chicken pox on Saturday, but I didn't. In the afternoon I went over to Felix's house. He wasn't contagious by now.

His mother let me in. Even though she was wearing ordinary workout clothes, there was something about the alert look on her face, her short, dark hair, her way of talking that let you know she didn't hang around the house lemon waxing the furniture.

Felix's father was different. He had—should I have been surprised?—red hair and freckles, and the same kind of pale blue eyes that Felix had. He shook my hand in a jock kind of way and kidded around for a while, but then he ambled off.

"Your dad . . . your folks . . . seem nice," I said to Felix when we were in his room.

"They're okay. So, Dan, you said one day you'd like some hands-on experience with a word processor. Should I guide you through the basics? Stop me if you already know what I'm showing you."

"Okay."

"Just give me time to boot it up."

What? Oh . . . turn it on. The language itself was confusing.

Felix went on punching keys and telling me about stuff like the status line, what information it showed, and other facts that began to blur. Then he said something I could really focus on.

"You may think, Dan, that computers are just for math and science things, but architects, guys like that, use them, too. So as an artist, you . . ."

I gave a shove to roll my chair back. "Hey, wait. I'm not an artist."

"Get outta here, of course you are. It's in your genes."

"No, it is not, Felix." I improvised. "Art usually skips a generation, so I'm safe."

"You're looney," he said. "So what are your career plans?"

"*Career plans?* Felix, I don't even know where I'm going to be living a year from now. Make that a month."

Felix picked up and leafed through a magazine. "You'll find a house."

"House? My folks don't want to stay in this town. They want to move to some godforsaken place up north."

Felix stared at me. "Why?"

"Because . . . because they're artists."

"Well, talk them out of it," Felix said.

As I was about to answer, the telephone rang.

Felix picked it up, said, "Who?" and looked pleased at whoever it was. The way he almost giggled, and talked in a fake, unnatural way, made me think it was a girl who'd called him.

After a bit he said, "Why don't you just ask him yourself? He's right here." He handed the phone to me.

Startled, I put my hand over the speaker and asked who it was.

Felix grinned. "You'll find out."

"Hello," I said, and when the girl replied, I asked, "Who is this?"

My chair rolled all by itself when she said, "Amanda."

"Amanda *who?*" I asked, so stupidly that Felix struck his forehead with the flat of his hand and rolled his eyes.

"Amanda Bowles," she said. "I called your grandmother's house and she said you were at Felix's. Doesn't he still have chicken pox?"

"No, he's going back to school," I said. "Why did you call me?"

Another stupid blunder. It sounded really rude, but it was too late now. I'd already said it.

"Well, I'm on the Snowfest committee. For next January?" she said.

"Right." As though I knew this.

"And we need to come up with some ideas for snow sculptures . . . every class does. And I wondered if you'd be on my committee?"

"Uh, well, I guess I can."

"That's great!" Pause. "Well, I'll talk to you later."

"Okay."

"Okay." Pause. "Bye, then."

"Bye." I hung up. "That was Amanda," I said to Felix.

"Oh, man, as if I didn't know. For the first time in my life I wish I was artistic instead of scientific. Dan . . ." Felix grabbed my arm dramatically. "Do anything, *anything* to stay in this town. I don't care what it takes. You've got too much going for you!"

"Right. I'll work on it." That was nonsense, and I knew it, but sometimes you say a thing just for the good feeling it gives you.

◆ ◆ ◆ ──────────────────────────

11

Stubborn Martha
Still Won't Talk

I got stuck taking care of Martha for longer hours so that Mom could have more peace and quiet to work on her paintings. One afternoon Martha was being brattier than usual, grabbing my school papers and bumping my elbow when I was trying to write. I gave up finally and told her to get one of her books; I'd read to her.

I was hoping she'd bring something I hadn't already read a trillion times, but naturally, she brought the beat-up copy of the book about a little teddy bear who got lost.

"Martha," I said, "don't you have a story with a little more suspense? Not too much sex and violence, of course, but a bone rattler? A blood chiller?"

For an answer, she gave me her *don't-mess-with-me* look and firmly pointed a chubby finger toward the cover.

I opened the book and began to read. She snatched it from me and jabbed that same chubby finger at the title.

Sighing, I read, "The Little Teddy Bear Who Got Losted."

She slapped my arm and gave me another of her looks.

"All right. 'The Little Teddy Bear Who Got *Lost*.' Satisfied?"

Then she pointed to the author's name so I'd read it, too. I think Grandma was the one who always read the title and author.

"Can we go on now?" I asked.

She nodded.

"*Yes, please, Dan, go on,*" I said in a childish voice (like hers would sound if she ever actually talked).

When I finished the story, I said, "*Thank you for reading to me. That was very nice,*" again in my childish voice. Naturally, it didn't register. Martha just scooted off the bed and raced from the room. I knew she was going to get another book.

Oh, not the one about the chick who didn't know its mother. Oh, please not that one, I thought. Martha could probably tell the whole story word for word. If she could talk. Or, rather, if she *would*.

The next day Felix wanted me to come to the town library with him after school. He liked the librarian, Mrs. Gayle, who could call in over the district-wide network for all kinds of books and magazines.

"Sorry, Felix, I can't," I said. "I have to go home and take care of Martha."

"Bring her along."

"Oh, you must be kidding. She'd tear up the joint."

"Nah. Besides, I think they have story times for little monsters. Come on, Dan."

When I led Martha into the room where the stories were going on, the youthful librarian looked at my sister doubtfully.

"She's awfully young," the woman said.

It did seem as if most of the kids were at least four or five.

"She won't be any problem," I said, my fingers crossed behind my back. "Martha loves stories."

"Ohhh," one of the little girls said, taking my sister's hand, "let her stay. She's so cute."

Martha *could* look cute when she wanted to. Right now, she had her head bent but was looking up shyly with her long-lashed eyes. Then she gave a little wiggle of her shoulders.

"All right, she can stay," the librarian said with a smile. Martha scooted down happily to the floor with the others, and I took off.

I found Felix at the front desk with a librarian who was typing into a computer. He turned as I came up.

"We've located a really neat source," he said. "A specialized library with all kinds of technical stuff."

The librarian looked at me and said, "Hi."

"This is Mrs. Gayle, who I've been telling you about," Felix said. And to her, "This is my friend Dan."

"Hi, Dan," she said. "I hear you're new in town. If you want to take out a card, the applications are over there." She turned back to the computer.

Her voice was so matter-of-fact . . . as if there was no question about my wanting a card . . . that I got the application and filled it out. Although I'm not superstitious in any way, I had the feeling that it could be a good sign for me to get a library card. It would state my intention, like driving in the first stake for a tent.

When she and Felix finished doodling around with the little screen, Mrs. Gayle took the application from me, read it, then looked up and smiled. "Are you by any chance Rachel Wakefield's son?"

"Yeah. Do you know her?"

"For years." She smiled even more and lowered her voice. "I used to baby-sit her."

I could only stare at the woman.

Felix laughed. "Hey, Dan, maybe Mrs. Gayle can slip you some inside info on what your mom was like as a kid. Some horrible things she did—"

"Never," Mrs. Gayle said. "Those are professional secrets. My lips are sealed."

"Oh . . . so there *were* things you could tell," Felix said, teasing. "Come on, Mrs. G. Just one little bitty—"

Putting a stop to it, Mrs. Gayle said to me, "Your mother was a very intelligent little girl, Dan. Even as a child she was quite talented. No one was surprised when she turned out to be a fine painter. Is she still working, by the way?"

"She's gone back to it," I said.

"Wonderful. Ask her to stop by some time, would you, Dan? It's great she's back in town. Maybe I can even coax her into doing some things for the library. When she has time, of course."

Mrs. Gayle didn't seem to expect an answer to all this. She had already turned to help some kids who'd come up to the desk.

As Felix and I walked away, I asked him if he'd told Mrs. Gayle we'd moved back to stay.

"Nah, we didn't talk about you. But maybe you will stay. You never know."

"Sure. And maybe it will snow radishes someday."

The little kids were straggling out of the story room, but I didn't see Martha. I went over to the door and looked in and almost fell on my face at what I heard. It was Martha. *Talking!*

"Thank you for reading to me," is what she was saying. "That was very nice." The very words I'd tried to put into her mouth at home—and failed!

"Why, sweetie, you're very welcome," the young librarian said, with an arm about Martha. "You must come back again."

"Okay, I will," my sister replied. The little creep! She could talk very well if she wanted to.

"Oh, look, here's your brother," the librarian said. "Now, come back again, will you . . . what's your name?"

Martha, after a quick look at me, went into her silent act again.

"Go on," I said. "Tell her your name." Would she do it? No.

"Her name's Esmerelda," I said.

Martha shot me a look but didn't contradict me.

"Well, Esmerelda is a big name for a little girl, isn't it?"

the librarian said. "My name is Jill. Now come back again, Esmerelda."

I didn't tell Felix about Martha's talking before we left the library, and I decided not to tell anyone at home, either. I was wondering how long Martha could keep up this silent routine. What a fake. All I did was not talk to her, either. We walked home together without a single word being said.

Mom asked Martha if she'd liked the library. Naturally, she didn't expect Martha to answer, and naturally, she didn't.

"Did she go to story hour?" Mom asked me.

"Ask her," I said.

Mom gave me a look. "I don't like that attitude, Dan."

I glanced at Martha, who was the picture of innocence. I was tempted to say she hated story hour and cried all the time. But if I did, that would mean I wouldn't be able to go back to the library, either. "Yeah, she went to story hour," I said.

That made me all the more determined not to tell anyone else about Martha being able to talk. Let them find out for themselves.

The trouble was, I realized later when we were eating, that everyone talked *for* Martha.

"Guess where our Martha went today?" Mom said, smiling fondly at her daughter, who was stuffing stuffed cabbage into her mouth. And before anyone could even wonder, Mom answered, "To the library. Didn't you, pet?"

Pet, of course, said nothing.

"And she heard a story, didn't you?" Mom went on. "I don't know what the story was about, though. Does anyone?"

My grandmother looked as though she couldn't care less. "Does anyone want bread? I forgot to put it on."

"I'll get it," I said and went to the kitchen. When I came back, they were talking about going somewhere.

"You don't intend to go there and come back the same day, do you?" my grandmother was saying. "It's farther than you might think, and there aren't any thruways when you get that far north."

Grandpa helped himself to bread. "You'll have to stay over somewhere," he said. "If the motels are open up there this time of year."

My mother gave a sharp little laugh. "You make it sound like some frozen outpost."

Grandpa just raised his eyebrows as though to say *It is.*

"What are you guys talking about?" I asked.

"We heard about a place for sale, and we may drive up to check it out," Dad said.

My heart sank. "What kind of place?"

"A summer cottage that's been winterized."

"*Cottage?*"

Mom finished wiping Martha's hands on a washcloth she always kept for that purpose. "It sounds great, Dan. The place it's in is a kind of art colony in the summer."

"What about winter?"

"Well . . ." Mom hesitated, but just for a second. "Someone has to make the first move toward changing it into a year-round place."

Grandma sighed. "Why does it have to be you, Rachel? And your family?"

Mom threw down the washcloth and stood up. "It never changes, does it?" she said. "All my life, anything I ever wanted to do, you could always find a reason not to!" She yanked Martha out of the high chair and stalked out of the room.

I felt sorry for Grandma. She sat there looking as though she'd been slapped. Then she got up and went to the kitchen.

There was a heaviness inside me, as if a bag of cement was weighing me down. Grandpa had a really sad expression. And my father . . . well, he looked like someone trapped.

12

What's a Library Sleepover?

E ven though there wasn't a story hour every day, I had to drag Martha along to the library with me. I decided to lay down some ground rules.

"Now, Martha," I said, "listen up. I'm taking you to the library, but that doesn't mean anyone's going to read to you. And it doesn't mean you have to hang around me all the time, either." I didn't like to think of what the guys might say if they saw me baby-sitting. "You got that?"

She looked up at me.

"Say 'yes,'" I told her. "No more of this silent act."

She stuck her chin out stubbornly. I stopped in the middle of the sidewalk. She looked at me and saw that I meant it. "Say 'yes.'"

She rolled her eyes, thinking. I took her hand and turned back toward home. She yanked her hand out of mine. "Yes!"

I felt like jumping up and down. I'd made her do it! I decided to press my luck. "Where are we going?" I asked.

She stuck her chin out again. "To the library."

That was more like it. What a feeling of power I suddenly had.

"What's your name?"

She gave me a dirty look.

"Is it Esmerelda?" I prodded.

"No! It's Martha! Let's go!"

All right. This was definitely something for me to be proud of. No one else in the family had ever gotten a word out of her.

At the library I sat Martha down at a little kid–size table and put a bunch of books in front of her.

"Stay here, now, until I come get you," I said. "Don't come looking for me. Understand?"

She didn't answer.

"Martha. Stay here. Okay? Answer me."

"*O-kay.*" She gave me another look, and I left.

I headed toward the desk to see if my library card was ready and almost zonked out. Amanda was coming through the door, with B.J. right behind her! Five minutes sooner and I'd have been caught playing nursie to old Martha.

"Hey!" B.J. greeted me.

"Hey," I said back.

"Hi, Dan," Amanda said.

"Hi, Amanda," I said back. Why did I always feel shy around her?

"You guys want to go watch a film?" B.J. asked.

"No," Amanda and I said together.

"Okay, you duds. Check you later," B.J. said, and left

Amanda and me standing near the door, not knowing what to say to each other. Finally I remembered what I was there for.

"I guess I'll go finalize my card," I said. I liked the sound of the word *finalize*.

"Oh, good." Amanda walked along with me, as though that's what she'd come to the library to do. It was fine with me.

"We've got to get together and talk about the Snow-fest," Amanda said. "I'll bet you'll come up with some hot ideas."

"Oh, right." Actually, I'd forgotten the Snowfest. I had decided there wasn't much point in even thinking about it. But I might as well pretend I'd still be around.

"There's plenty of time," Amanda said. We were up at the desk by now. "The big sleepover comes up first."

"The *what?*"

Amanda wrinkled her pretty forehead. "Hasn't anyone even told you about the library sleepover?"

I could only shake my head. Just then Mrs. Gayle came over. "Hi, Amanda. What can I do for you?"

"Is my mother's poetry book here?" Amanda asked.

"Oh, yes." Mrs. Gayle searched beneath the circulation counter and found a thin book with a reserve slip in it.

As she was processing the book, Amanda asked, "Has the date been set for the sixth-grade sleepover?"

"Yes, it's a weeknight during the holiday break. Your teacher will fill you in on the exact details."

"What is the sleepover, anyway?" I asked.

"It's something we started a couple of years ago," Mrs.

Gayle said. "We have different nights during the school term when a whole class spends a night reading and telling stories here at the library. It makes the staff crazy, but we love it."

"You mean . . . all night?"

"Yes, it's great!" Amanda said. "We bring sleeping bags and stake out our spots. The library even gives us snacks and breakfast."

"And anyone who wants to can come to it?" I asked.

"So long as you're a working member of your class and have a library card," Mrs. Gayle said. "No nonreaders allowed. See, Dan, you showed good judgment by signing up when you did. Now you're eligible!"

After Amanda and I walked away from the desk, we started to talk about the sleepover and then Amanda smiled and said, "Oh, how cute!"

I turned around and then turned to jelly. It was Martha. And she was toddling right over to us.

"Who's this little sweetie pie?" Amanda asked as Martha came and stood by me. "Is she your sister, Dan?"

"Yeah. I had to bring her along because . . ."

"Mommy made him bring me," Martha said. I might have known that when she talked, she'd say something to embarrass me.

Amanda stooped down to Martha's level. "What's your name?" she asked.

Martha darted a look at me. "It's Esmerelda," I said.

"My name is Martha!"

"Martha, eh. Well, you're a real doll, Martha."

Amanda stood up and gave a little smile. "Now I understand why you have those mittens around your neck, Dan."

"What!" I could have died standing there. I *wanted* to die standing there. When I'd sat Martha down at the table and taken off her snowsuit, I must have put her mittens-on-a-string around my neck and forgotten to take them off! What could I say?

"Don't you think they go well with my eyes?" I said, which made no sense at all.

Amanda just laughed. "I never noticed before, but your eyes *are* a peculiar shade of pink." I could laugh then, because I could tell she wasn't making fun of me.

At that moment, wouldn't you know, B.J. had to come along. "There's no way I'm sitting all the way through *The Sound of Music,*" she said.

"If you're leaving, I'll walk along with you." Amanda pulled on her gloves.

B.J. looked a bit surprised but shrugged and said, "Suit yourself."

She ought to be nicer when someone reaches out, I thought. Especially someone as great as Amanda. But maybe B.J. just didn't care about having friends.

Amanda said good-bye to Martha and me, and left with B.J. I stooped and got Martha into her snowsuit. She made a fuss when I told her she couldn't take her stack of books along.

One of the library helpers, clearing off the table, said, "You can check them out for her if you have a card."

Great. I could now walk out of there with a little kid

and an armful of baby books. Still, I checked them out, knowing Martha would howl all the way home if I didn't.

I was lucky. As we walked home, I saw only one kid ahead of us, lugging a bag of groceries.

"Thank you for getting the books for me," I said, meaning that Martha should repeat the words.

"You're welcome," she said.

At home, Martha still acted as if she couldn't talk. I decided not to blow her cover. I would wait for just the right time to do it.

*

I called Felix after supper that night and asked him what he knew about the sleepover.

"Hey, I forgot that's coming up," he said. "It's a real howl. Be sure you sign up for it. Did you find out the date?"

"No, just that it's a weeknight during Christmas vacation." I crossed my fingers, hoping that nothing would keep me from going. "Were you there last year?"

"Of course. It was such a blast. One of the guys—oh-oh. I'll tell you later. A living pestilence just walked into the room."

"A *what*?"

"A germ invasion named B.J."

"She's there now?" What was she doing, hanging around Felix's house at seven in the evening?

"Yeah, her mom's working late."

"I see. And you're her sitter?"

"Yeah, Dan, I'm B.J.'s baby-sitter, that's right!" He

laughed, and then I could hear him telling B.J. to stop pounding on him.

"C'mon, Felix," I said, "tell me about the sleepover. What happened?"

"One of the guys got his brother to sneak outside and go up to a window and jiggle one of those cardboard Halloween skeletons—wait a minute, Dan." Then I heard him taunting B.J. "Oh, you were too scared, you sissy. I saw you leap right into the arms of Harvey Jones—ouch!"

There were sounds of scuffling, and then Felix shouted, "Don't you dare!" At last there was a loud bang, like a door closing, and then Felix came back on the phone. "That creep pulled the plug on my computer! I've gotta see if I can retrieve some stuff. Talk to you later, okay?"

"Okay." I hesitated. "Felix, if you and B.J. fight so much, why do you let her hang around?"

There was a pause and then Felix said, "Well, Dan, I really can't do anything about that. It's one of those things. You know?"

"Right." But I didn't know. Just one of *what* things?

The cardboard skeleton caper seemed third-gradish, but the sleepover itself sounded like a major blast. I'd never heard of any library doing that before. This town had a lot going for it.

I felt keyed up. I wanted to know more about the sleepover, but the only kid I knew well enough to call was Amanda. And I didn't know her that well.

Okay, I'd do it. I'd call her and talk very casually, the way guys did on TV shows.

I picked up the phone and dialed Amanda's number,

but before it could even ring once, I hung up. What would I say? How would I begin . . . ? Well, how about, *Hi, Amanda, what's happening?* No. *Hi, Amanda, guess who?* No. Just *Hi, Amanda, this is Dan.* I picked up the phone and jumped at a voice behind me.

It was Mom. "Dan," she said, "what are you mumbling about?"

Was I mumbling? "Nothing," I said.

"Were you going to make another call, or could I use the phone now?"

"Oh. Go ahead." I reached over, and with the cuff of my sweater wiped the phone where it had gotten a little sweaty. "Who are you calling, Mom?" I said it just to seem calm.

"The people who own the cottage. We want to drive up to see it before the weather gets any worse."

Great. And just when I was feeling good, looking ahead, making plans.

As for the sleepover, right then I believed I'd still be in town for it about as much as I believed in the tooth fairy. As much as I believed I'd ever have anything even close to a normal, school-kid kind of life.

13

Mom's One-Time Baby-sitter

The next week, on the library's story hour day, I walked home from school thinking I'd take Martha.

Maybe Amanda would show up at the library again. If she did, I'd search for some art books on statues as though I was looking for inspiration for the snow sculpture. There was always . . . barely . . . a chance that we'd still be here for the January Snowfest. If we were, I could impress Amanda and her committee with some sensational ideas.

I walked into the kitchen and stared.

"What is it?" Mom asked, staring back.

"You've got real clothes on."

Mom rolled her eyes, finished some fruit juice, and turned to rinse the glass. "Okay, so I'm dressed up."

She wasn't all that dressed up, actually. Only instead of her usual paint-stained shirt and jeans with holes in the knees, she had on a sweater and a full skirt that came down to her boots.

"You look great," I said. "I like your hair that way." She'd pulled it back and put it in a kind of pigtail.

"You like it?" Mom smiled, pleased. "It's called a French braid. I used to wear it this way when I went out on dates with your dad." She turned to call Martha. Then to me she said, "I've got to go to the health food store and get some whole wheat flour and molasses. We're almost out."

"I was going to take Martha to the library, to story hour," I said.

"Oh, that's sweet, Dan." Mom ran her hand along my cheek and gave it a little pat. "You're such a good kid. I know I don't show it, but I do appreciate you."

Then she gave me a hug, and I hugged her back.

"I was planning to go anyway," I said. "To do some research."

"Oh? What do you need to research?"

Amanda. "Some art stuff."

"Really?" Anything to do with art pleased Mom. "Well, maybe I'll go with you. I haven't been to that library in just ages."

Oh, no. But what could I say? Now I was hoping Amanda wouldn't show up. First I'm with my baby sister, and now I'd be with her and my *mother.* How embarrassing! "Okay," I said. "Maybe I'll see you there." I could always duck out of sight if Amanda walked in.

"No, honey, come along with me. The grocery things might be a little heavy, and with Martha . . ."

So a little later, after going to the store, we walked into the library together, Martha, Mom, and me. I showed Mom where the story hour was held, and after she dropped off the kid, we went over to the counter, where Mrs. Gayle greeted Mom with open arms.

"It's wonderful to see you again after all these years!" Mrs. Gayle said. "I've kept up with you through clippings and art news now and then. I'm just so proud of you!"

Mom stood there, a little flushed but looking very pleased.

"I always knew you had a special talent," the librarian went on. "I still have a couple of your drawings, framed, hanging in my bedroom."

"Oh, really," Mom said. I'd never seen her eyes sparkle like that. "Well, maybe I should let you see what I've been doing lately."

She went on to describe her work, and I looked around. No sign of Amanda. What a relief.

I remembered that I was supposed to be doing research, so I wandered over to the art book section and took down a few volumes. One of them had some pretty neat statues . . . not people, but geometrical shapes that wouldn't be too hard to replicate. Then I started thinking . . . snow cones . . . those shaved ice drinks for summer with colored flavors. Could we color snow? And put little reflectors on it here and there . . . and attach little lights? Only they'd have to be cool lights that wouldn't melt the snow.

Wow. I started sketching copies of some of the better designs and noting the book titles and page numbers. I'd never copy them exactly. No artist would stoop that low. But there was nothing wrong in getting inspiration from something or someone else. Painters, artists, all kinds of creative people did that.

Whoa. What was this? I was thinking like an *artist*. Me,

who would never be an artist even if . . . well, I never would be, that's all.

Just then Mom and Mrs. Gayle strolled by.

"What's that you're drawing, Dan?" Mom had to ask.

"Just something for a school project."

"Mrs. Gayle is taking me on a tour of the library, Dan. I had no idea they had all these resources!"

"Oh, we keep up," Mrs. Gayle said. "Right now we're very much involved with environmental issues."

That remark set off a bell in Mom's head. I could almost hear the *ping*. "Really! Here at the library?" she asked.

"Yes, we have monthly meetings. There's a good turn-out, and we're divided into committees."

"What issues are you involved in?" Mom asked, sliding into a chair. I guessed the rest of the tour could wait.

Mrs. Gayle, after a look at the desk to see how busy it was, sat down, too. "Well, with the lake and all the activities on it . . . boating, sailing, and in the winter, snowmobiling . . . we have to keep a watch so it doesn't get polluted."

"Oh! They'd just better not pollute Lake Lorraine!" Mom said. "It's a gorgeous lake. I have so many great girlhood memories . . ."

"Exactly. And we want to keep it that way for our children and their children. Would you be interested in joining the group, Rachel? As an artist you have a greater stake than most people."

"Oh, sure, I'll do anything I can do to help. For as long as we're here, of course."

"You mean you're not here to stay?" Mrs. Gayle said. "I assumed . . ."

"Oh, no, we're moving up north, into the wilds." Mom gave a little laugh.

"The wilds? What do you mean?"

"We're looking for a place where nature's undisturbed. We want the real thing, back to the earth . . ." Mom faltered a little at the look on Mrs. Gayle's face. "We want our children to be able to enjoy nature."

"I'm sure many parents do," Mrs. Gayle said. "But to pick up and move to the wilderness . . . it seems . . ."

"It seems what?"

Mrs. Gayle shrugged. "Like an escape. Picking up and going where it's unspoiled instead of staying where you are and helping preserve the environment we have right around us."

Mom flushed a little but set her chin the way she did when she insisted on having her own way. "We're made the decision, my husband and I."

Mrs. Gayle kept her voice pleasant. "Michael's a teacher, isn't he?"

"Yes. Art. For college students, though right now he's substituting in one of the high schools."

"Will he continue . . . I mean, will there be colleges where you're going?"

"It depends on where we settle. He can always commute, you know. Or stay in a college town during the school week and come home on weekends. Our plans aren't set. They can always change."

"For the worse," I muttered, over the big art book.

I could tell Mom heard that and was looking at me, but she didn't say anything.

"Rachel," Mrs. Gayle said, "since you might be here for a while, I wonder if you'd like to put some of your work into a gallery for possible sales? A terrific new one just opened in town, and the owner told me she's looking for a fine artist."

Mom acted casual, but I could tell she was interested by the little quiver in her cheek. "Whose gallery is it?"

"Dottie Hanson's. She's fairly new in town. I've got her card somewhere. Would you like it?"

Mom shrugged. "All right. But I really doubt . . ."

I don't know why Mom always has to put on these airs. I was waiting for her to say she wouldn't turn her paintings over to any kind of schlock shop.

Just then the little kids came streaming out of story hour. One little girl was holding Martha's hand. My sister saw Mom and broke away and came toward us, but as usual she didn't say a word.

"Hi, sweetheart," Mom said. "Were the stories good?"

Martha took hold of Mom's wrist and pulled her arm, as though she wanted to go back to the story room.

"But, honey," Mom said, "they're all over now. You'll have to wait until next week for more."

"I'll bet she wants you to see the animals," Mrs. Gayle said. "All the kids love them." She went back toward the desk, and Mom and I followed Martha to the other room.

"Oh, little bunnies," Mom said, stopping at the first cage. "Aren't they sweet? Maybe some day you can raise rabbits, baby."

"We could probably use the fur," I said. "In the frozen North."

Mom gave me a withering look and moved to some farther cages that contained gerbils. She didn't seem quite so thrilled by them, but she wasn't thrilled at all by the contents of the last two cages. "Snakes! They allow snakes in a children's room?"

"They're harmless, Mom."

"Martha! No!" Mom rushed at my sister, who was trying to open one of the snake cages. She grabbed Martha's wrist. "They should keep these locked instead of having latches any child could open." She stooped to Martha's level. "You must not open these cages ever, Martha. Understand?"

Martha stuck out her lower lip. We all knew that expression. It meant, *I understand, but I don't like it.*

Mom stood up. "All right, let's get going," she said.

As we went by the desk, Mrs. Gayle said, "Rachel, here's Dottie's card and some information on our preserve-the-environment goals. I hope you'll join us for as long as you're in town."

Mom put the papers in her purse and smiled. But I knew she was a little ticked at the librarian for what she'd said about sticking around and cleaning up where you live instead of just moving away.

There were Christmas decorations in the stores now, and some homes even had colored lights blazing away. It felt like Christmas. The air was really chill, and the gray clouds hanging low in the sky could bring snow.

When we walked into the kitchen, a great smell came

rolling out at us. "Mmmm," I said, "what's cooking, Grandma?"

"Pot roast," she said. "With carrots, potatoes, brussels sprouts, tomatoes . . ."

"Sound good, except for the brussels sprouts," I said.

"Except for the meat," Mom said. She took the bag from me and put the contents on the counter. Whole wheat flour, molasses, wheat germ, oat bran, sunflower seeds. A yucky bunch of so-called food. "I guess," Mom said, taking off her coat and helping Martha out of hers, "that I can't make my whole wheat muffins with the oven already in use."

"I guess not," Grandma said. She gave me a wink. "Such a disappointment for all of us."

"Did anyone call for me?" I asked.

"Yes, Felix. Is he all over the chicken pox now?"

"Oh, sure."

"Did many children come down with it?"

I took an apple from the fruit bowl. "Nope. Just Felix and B.J."

As I headed toward the stairs, I heard Grandma murmur to Mom, "That's a strange setup, even for these days. . . ."

Mom said, "Yes, but with K.K. nothing surprises me."

I had no idea what they were talking about. What strange setup? And who was K.K.?

I used the phone in my grandparents' room, as I always did when I was upstairs. "Felix? You called?"

"Yo. Where were you, Christmas shopping?"

"Not yet. What's up?"

"I wanted to share some input about the sleepover. We should get there early, to stake out the best spot."

"What's the best spot?"

"As close to Shirley and Traci as we can get."

I might have known.

Felix went on, "Dan, I don't want to come across as macho, but in case some feeble wit tries a scare tactic like last year, I want to be there for the girls."

"Sure, Felix. You still like both of them, huh?"

"Yeah. I wish I could decide which is the winner and which the runner-up, but they're both such foxes. You see my dilemma."

"It's a tough call," I agreed.

I couldn't help wishing something wild would happen at the sleepover and Amanda would rush to me for protection. But she impressed me as a girl who was very much in control. It would take a whole lot more than a stupid cardboard skeleton to make her come unglued.

14

It Takes a Monster to Know One

Two weeks before Christmas, the best trees on the lot had been sold. All of the decorations Mom and Grandma's friend had made had been snapped up, too.

"If I hadn't been teaching, we could have gone up a week ago and got another big load of trees," my dad said.

"We did all right," Grandpa said. "Anyway, from now till Christmas lots of people will go and chop down their own trees."

"They ought to dig them up by the roots," my mother observed, "so they could plant them later."

"Not in my house, thank you very much," Grandma said. "I don't need to have dirt dragged in in a huge root ball."

That wouldn't be a problem. Our tree stood in a bucket of water by the garage.

The grown-ups were doing some shopping, bringing in packages that disappeared from sight immediately. I had a little money for presents myself from my birthday and baby-sitting. Mom had insisted that I take it. She'd said that because I'd kept Martha out of her hair, she'd been able to do lots of nature paintings.

Mom had checked out the Dottie Hanson Gallery that Mrs. Gayle had told her about. When she saw that all of the crafts and art objects in the place were made by some of the most respected artists in the Midwest, Mom decided to let the gallery handle her own work. Her paintings sold like crazy.

The next Wednesday after school, Mom asked if I'd go with her and Martha to deliver two new watercolors to the gallery.

"Why can't I just stay here with the kid?" I countered.

"She needs the outing," Mom said. "Besides, there's a toy shop right next door to the gallery. I thought you could take Martha there, see what she likes, and then I could slip in and get it while you two walk on home."

We had just reached the gallery when B.J. strolled up with someone who could have been her older sister, except that she looked more put together.

To my surprise, Mom said, "Well, K.K., I haven't seen you in ages!"

"Rachel," the older girl said, eyeing Mom. "My kid told me you were back in town."

And then I realized this was B.J.'s mother! She did look older, once I got a close look at her.

"They were in the same class," B.J. muttered to me. "They hated each other's guts."

I doubted it was that bad, but I could tell from the polite tones and the sizing-up looks the two women were giving each other that they'd never got along.

"What are you up to these days, K.K.?" my mom asked.

"I'm up to my you-know-what in real estate. As a matter of fact, this gallery was one of the properties I handled. I got Dottie and the owner together and laid out a deal."

"You were always so good at that," my mom said.

I'm sure that Mom was thinking K.K. looked like a phony in her fringed leather coat and pants, and with her hair pulled back to show off some heavy-duty silver earrings. And K.K. probably thought Mom looked too artsy in that long skirt, turtleneck sweater, and cape, with her hair just streaming all around.

"So, have you come to settle down in the old hometown after all?" K.K. asked, with a wicked little smile.

"Actually, no," Mom said. "We're just stopping over. We'll soon be moving north of here."

"North where?"

"You've probably never heard of it. It's in upper Minnesota, Sleeping Waters."

"Hey, I sold a couple of cottages there! But why would you go to a place like that now? It's a summer resort. There's nobody there in the winter."

Mom's mouth opened a little. "You must be mistaken. We heard of a place . . ."

K.K. shook her head, laughing. "You've been misinformed. Believe me, that place closes down in off-season. Even the one little store and the laundromat and the filling station are closed."

B.J., who'd been taking this all in, piped up, "Lucky you, Dan! No school!"

For the first time, K.K. seemed to notice Martha and me. "These your kids?"

"Yes," Mom said. She looked a little stunned.

"You weren't planning on taking them—?"

"Kitty, they *are* my children, and I certainly intend to take them." She turned to me. "Dan, why don't you go along with Martha to the toy store and do what I asked you. I'll see you back home."

B.J. said to her mother, "I'm gonna hang out with Dan."

K.K. fished some keys out of a fringed leather bag, tossed them to B.J., and said, "Wait in the car when you're through. I'll be along eventually."

As we walked away, B.J. said, "Want to go for a little spin?"

"Not now," I said, refusing to react. I wouldn't have put it past her to know how to drive. "Does your mom have a real name?"

"Katherine Kay. She's sharp-looking, isn't she?"

"Very nice, yes."

"Your mom looks good, too, in her own way."

"I'll tell her you said so." I meant that to be sarcastic, like, *Oh, my mom will be so thrilled to hear that you think she looks good, your opinion counts for so much,* but B.J. just smiled.

The toy store was crowded, which wasn't surprising this time of year.

"I suppose she wants to see the goony dolls," B.J. said. "They're over there."

But Martha brushed right past the dolls and went on to a section of windup monster creatures.

"All right! The kid's got taste!" B.J. said. "Hey, Martha, let me wind this one up for you. How do you like that, huh?"

The thing, which was about ten inches high, staggered forward, arms clutching and mouth opening to shoot out sparks.

Martha made a grab for it.

"No, don't touch it!" I told her. "Just look."

"Oh, go on, let her play with it," B.J. said. "They put out these things for samples. They know kids are gonna break a few." She wound up some others.

Martha was so fascinated with the creatures that when I said we had to go, she clutched the edge of the shelf and tried to kick me away.

"You've got to come with me now if you expect Santa to bring you one of these," I said, dodging her feet and prying away her fingers.

"The kid really relates to monsters," B.J. noted approvingly.

"Yeah, well, it takes one to know one," I said as I finally managed to drag my sister away from the spark-shooting creatures.

15

What Not to Do
at a Sleepover

I t wasn't until about a week before we were to get out for Christmas vacation that our homeroom teacher told us about the library sleepover.

"The school has pledged cooperation," she said, "but that doesn't include the ultimate sacrifice . . . being there to supervise."

The class cheered.

"However," Miss Hawthorne said, raising a hand for silence, "that doesn't mean you're not going to *be* supervised."

The class groaned.

"They're asking for parent volunteers. Do any of you feel that your mother or father would be willing to spend the night with you people?"

Silence. I turned around to see if anyone was stupid enough to raise a hand. Everyone else was looking around to check out the same thing.

The teacher gave a grudging kind of smile. "All right, I can see no one wants his or her own parent present. But someone has to be there. We can't ask the library staff to do it. So think about it. Ask at home. And let me know."

We talked about it at lunch hour, Felix, Amanda, B.J., Traci, Shirley, and Todd. And me. None of us wanted to have the night ruined by having a parent around.

Felix pointed his fork at B.J. "Your mom's pretty freewheeling," he said. "She wouldn't care what we did. Think she'd agree?"

B.J. washed down a disgusting mouthful of food with an orange drink. "K.K. would rather walk down Elm Street stark naked than spend a night with a bunch of sixthgraders. No way, Fruit-O-Lay."

"How about your mom, Amanda?"

"No, she's busy."

"It could be a father, you know," Traci said. "Like, my dad wouldn't care what anyone did. He lets my sister and brother tear up the house when my mom's out."

"Get him, get him!" we all said.

"My mom falls asleep during thunderstorms, horror movies on TV, anything. So she wouldn't be good as a supervisor," Todd said.

"She'd be *perfect!*" Felix yelled, and we all agreed. "Waste no time. Ask her today. Sign her up!" everyone urged Todd.

A couple of days later, Mrs. Hawthorne told us three parents had signed up. "Todd's mother and Traci's father and also Kate's father." She sounded relieved.

"Now, class, here's the routine," she continued. "You're to go to the library sometime around five. You will take your sleeping bag, nightclothes . . . and here they've added a note." She lowered her glasses, gave us a look, and pushed back the glasses to read: " 'The library may get chilly during the night—heat is automatically controlled—so students are urged to wear appropriately warm nightwear and bring along bedroom slippers.' "

There was a murmur in the back of the room. Mrs. Hawthorne looked up and said, "What was that, Josh?"

Everyone turned to stare at him. He looked down, looked up, and grinned. "I just said that instead of bedroom slippers, they could wear sleepers with feet in them."

"Wonderful," Mrs. Hawthorne commented. "Do wear yours, Josh, if that's what you're used to." He squirmed when everyone laughed.

"Let's get on with this. 'At six o'clock students will eat a sack supper, which they will bring from home. This will be followed by individual reading. At nine o'clock, parent supervisors will arrive. There will be reading aloud for an hour and a half or so, followed by free-time talk and moving about.' "

Mrs. Hawthorne gave us that glasses-down-on-the-nose look again and said, "You know, people, they're treating you with respect, so I'm sure *you'll* respect the rules and keep the moving about down to windstorm energy, not a full-blown tornado."

No one said a word. Mouths were kept tight shut, but eyes had a lot of movement. *Sure, sure,* is what the eyes were saying.

"There's not much more. 'Pizza will be brought in at nine o'clock,' " . . . and above the shouts of the kids, "'courtesy of the Friends of the Library, and then there will be individual reading until midnight, when all lights go out!'"

The kids murmured about how great it was, up until midnight, when the guy behind me whispered, "They hope we'll be worn out by then. Good luck."

"Okay," Mrs. Hawthorne said. "Just this final note. 'There will be no need for flashlights. And please, no sweet treats—unless you wish to supply everyone, including the hardworking library staff.'"

The kids laughed, and then Mrs. Hawthorne added, "It ends with '*Please, please, no chewing gum.*' Now, people, I suggest you abide by this rule. You know why it's been made. Remember, the library is doing all this out of the goodness of its heart, and your response will show whether or not they'll repeat the sleepover night. Okay?"

Later I asked Felix how come no gum.

"Oh, man, last year a couple of retrobrains crawled around during lights out and stuck gum in some girls' hair. It was not a pretty sight."

'Why no flashlights?"

"Again, some idiots would crawl up and shine the light smack into someone's face. Or shine it onto someone leaving to go to the washroom so everyone would know. Real retarded things like that. I just used mine to read."

"After lights out, you mean?"

"Oh, sure. Some others did, too. We kept the lights down in our sleeping bags. It didn't bother anyone, but now . . . because of those guys . . ."

"How many kids do you think will be there?"

"As many as there are in our class. Thirty-one. No one wants to miss out on it."

"I can't wait." It sounded like more fun than Christmas. Which was coming up fast.

*

The tree Grandpa had picked out for us was in its stand in the living room now, waiting to be decorated. Taking advantage of Martha's nap time, Grandma brought out several boxes of old ornaments and put them on the sofa.

Mom had a glow on her face as she looked at them. "I remember this!" she exclaimed as she held up a round red ball covered with holly leaves. "I painted it when I was about six years old. Look, Dan!"

"Yeah, nice."

"Oh . . . and these!" Mom, kneeling on the floor, held up two frail-looking lions. "We've had these as long as I can remember!"

"They belonged to *my* mother," Grandma said. "Someday they'll be yours, and then your children's."

After the tree was all trimmed, we sat back while Grandma turned on the lights. "It's gorgeous," she said. "You did a perfect job, Rachel and Dan." She lowered her voice. "You know, Grandpa thinks he's the only one who can arrange the lights. Well, you showed him, didn't you?"

"We sure did," Mom said.

We heard voices and Grandpa called out, "Where is everybody?"

"In here, in the living room," Grandma answered.

He and Dad walked in, with Dad holding Martha, who'd just come down the stairs. She stopped rubbing her eyes when she saw the tree all lit up. Her mouth formed an O.

I almost expected my sister to break down and say something in front of the family at last, but she didn't. And then I got a super idea. I'd coach her to say "Merry Christmas" on Christmas Eve! That would blow everyone's socks off and give them a gift no amount of money could buy!

"I'll bet Martha doesn't remember Christmas last year," Grandpa was saying.

"Oh, of course not." Dad took her a step closer to the tree.

"I hope she remembers this one," Mom said.

"If not this one, then others to follow." Grandma kissed Martha's hand. "Next year you'll be a big girl, won't you?"

"Don't count on our being here," Mom said. "Who knows? We could be snowbound the whole winter."

There was a chill in the room right then. After a frozen silence, Grandma said, "I've got to check on that chicken," and left for the kitchen. Grandpa started to say something to my mom but settled on a look and a sigh before he left, too.

"Honey," Dad said softly to my mother, "do you have to keep reminding them, just when they're feeling good?" He put Martha down.

"If I don't, they'll act as though we're going to stay here forever."

"They just love having the family around. You should be glad of that."

"All right, I'm glad they want us," Mom said, reaching to move an ornament higher up on the tree. "But that doesn't change things. We're going up to look at that place right after Christmas. I've called. I told you I was going to."

"I know." Dad sounded resigned.

"So it's all set." Mom's jaw was also set.

"Mom . . ." I began.

"What?"

By her tone, this didn't sound like a good time, but I plunged ahead anyway. "If there's nothing around up there in the winter, how far would I have to ride to school?"

"I don't know." And then she dropped the clinker. "I've decided to teach you at home, anyway. So there's no problem."

No problem! Growing up ignorant is not a problem? I'd be like Daniel Boone in the wilderness, only without the fur cap. Naturally, wearing animal skins was another no-no.

I couldn't believe this was actually going to happen. Wasn't there some way out?

16.

◆ ◆ ◆ ――――――――――――

The Mysterious Wolf Watch

Feeling as depressed as I did about my future life (if you could call it a life), I couldn't raise much of a Christmas spirit.

When anyone asked me what I wanted, I told them it didn't matter. Anything good was electronic, and what use would that be if we were living in some hut? I didn't have to ask for warm clothes. I knew I'd get them anyway.

When I was out shopping one day with Felix, he went into a women's clothing store and bought his mom a pair of mules, which in spite of the dumb name were really bedroom slippers. They consisted of soles, really high heels, and some fluffy stuff in front. Of course they were black.

"Hot stuff, huh?" Felix said to me. "Why don't you get your mom a pair, too?"

"My mom?" I couldn't help breaking up.

Felix looked puzzled. "You mean she wouldn't be thrilled?"

I shook my head. "If my mom isn't going barefoot, she wears thick socks, sometimes with leg warmers. Oh, and for special occasions she has this old beat-up pair of moccasins with most of the beads missing."

"But maybe she'd like a change."

I shook my head some more. But for a moment I was tempted. It would be worth buying those mules just to see the expression on Mom's face. Only I didn't have that kind of money.

"Maybe I'll get some mousetraps," I told him. "Paint them with gold, glue sequins on them, tie on ribbons. For when we're living in the wild."

"Hey, man, don't talk like that. Think positively. Maybe your parents will change their minds at the last minute."

"Yeah, Felix. There's as much chance of that as of an astronaut saying at blast-off time, 'Hey, you know, gang, let's do this some other time.'"

Felix gave me a look that made me feel like a real whiner, but then he put his hand on my shoulder. "Try to keep up your spirits, old man. Maybe we can think of something."

"Okay. Sorry." I really didn't want to spoil Felix's day.

At the toy store I bought one of the monsters for Martha. I knew Mom and Dad wouldn't. Felix and I spent quite a bit of time messing around the store, pretending we were kids who wanted stuff. Felix was a real cutup. He picked up a toy giraffe and said loudly that he wanted Santa to bring him one just like it. Several little kids stood and stared at him before their parents, giving Felix disgusted looks, tugged them away.

"Was it something I said?" Felix called after them.

"Come on, let's get out of here," I said.

As we walked down the street, Felix told me he had just one more thing to buy. "Maybe you don't want to hang around," he said.

"No, that's okay. I have time."

"Well, this may bore you. It's something I have to get for a girl."

"Really?" The last I knew, Felix still liked both Traci and Shirley. I wondered when he'd made the cut. "Which girl?"

"You know."

"No, I don't."

"Come on, Dan, you've heard kids talk at school."

"They don't talk much around me. I'm still the new kid, remember?"

Felix turned up his collar against the cold. "What about your mom? Hasn't she ever said anything?"

"About what?" Why would my mother *care*?

"About B.J. and me."

"You and B.J.?" Now I was totally confused. We'd reached the department store, and Felix, who'd obviously been there before, walked to a display of holograms.

"I guess I'll get her one of these watches with a wolf's head." He turned it back and forth to make the face change from an eerie orange to a bright green. "Think she'll like it?"

"It's very sweet. Felix . . . what is all this about you and B.J.? I don't get it."

"Look, as long as you really don't know, I'll tell you about it sometime, but not now. Okay?"

"Sure." There were quite a few shoppers around us, so I decided not to press the matter.

The price on the watch was plainly visible. I wondered how Felix could afford a gift like this. He used a credit card. It had his father's name on it.

"Won't your dad find out?" I whispered, as the clerk filled out the forms.

"Sure, when I give him the receipt. That's all he cares about, to have the receipts to check against the credit card bill when it comes. Okay, let's go," he said, shoving the package into his jacket pocket.

As we walked along, I wondered why Felix's father wouldn't mind paying for a watch for some girl. And why Felix would want to give a gift to B.J., of all people. As far as I knew, all she'd ever given him was chicken pox.

Before I could think of a casual way of asking, Felix said, taking a deep breath, "It's really nice out here on the street now, with all the colored lights and decorations."

"Yeah. Nice. Do you guys have your tree up yet?"

"No. It's just a high-tech aluminum number anyway, one that folds up. Last year we decorated it with computer chips."

"Well, do you . . . like . . . hang up stockings? No, I guess you wouldn't," I answered myself. "It's pretty childish. I wouldn't either, except for Martha. You have to do that stuff when there are little kids around."

"That's really nice," Felix said.

"Yeah, but I really don't like getting up at the crack of

dawn and unwrapping presents when I'm half awake. I guess that all changes when you stop believing in Santa."

"I never did believe," Felix said. "My parents used to take me out and buy me what I wanted, and that was that."

We'd reached the corner where we split off to go in opposite directions. Felix stopped, shoved his hands deeper into his pockets, and said, "I'd like to hear about everything you do at your house on Christmas."

"Fine, but not now," I said. "It's freezing. How about if I call you?"

"Good." Felix started off and then turned and caught up with me. "I've got a great idea," he said. "You could borrow our camcorder and film everything you do. Wouldn't that be neat?"

"I guess. We'll talk about it." I was really shivering. Felix didn't look all that cold, but then he was wearing a sheepskin jacket and earmuffs.

As I crunched along the snowy walk toward home, I thought about how lucky Felix was to have everything he wanted. But then I saw him as he'd been just now, blue eyes watering from the cold, nose pink and also a little watery, asking me about our Christmas. As if he'd never had one. It did sound as though he'd never had a normal holiday. Even ours last year, when Mom had trimmed the tree with chili peppers instead of cranberries, had a Christmas kind of feeling.

And just as I got to the front yard and saw our Christmas tree through the window, its colored lights reflecting outside on the snow, I got the brilliant idea. I'd have Felix over to share our celebration! He could see for himself what it was like, instead of hearing about it secondhand or watching some amateur movie.

After I put away the presents I'd bought, I went down to the living room, where Mom and Grandma were sitting around talking. Besides the Christmas tree there now were fat, pine-scented candles with red bows on end tables, and a little village with cotton snow on the coffee table. The whole feeling of the room was warm and festive. I thought of Felix in his cold, black-and-white house and felt really sad for him.

Without planning to, I blurted, "Grandma, would you mind if Felix spent Christmas with us?"

"*Dan!*" Mom said in her mind-your-manners tone.

"Darling," Grandma said, looking puzzled, "your friends are always welcome, but on a holiday wouldn't Felix miss being with his own family?"

"Not at all. They don't celebrate."

"Don't celebrate?" Grandma looked more puzzled than ever. "Is it for religious reasons?"

"Oh, no. They just can't be bothered. Felix's folks give him a charge card and tell him to get what he wants. And their tree is aluminum, trimmed with computer chips."

"Now, really," Grandma said. "That's just—"

"And because he doesn't know what a real family get-together is like, he asked me to videotape our celebration. He has a camcorder."

"Of course. He would have," my mother said, not too kindly.

"Mom, don't blame Felix!"

"I'm not. I'm blaming his father." And to my grand-mother, "That Arthur always did have a strange sense of values." She lifted her eyebrows a little. "In every way. Did I tell you I ran into K.K. the other day?"

"Later, Rachel," my grandmother said. I knew by the tone of her voice there was something they knew that they didn't want me to know. "Dan," Grandma said, "forget the movie taking. Just tell Felix to come on over and see for himself. We can certainly do that much for him." And to my mother, "I can't believe . . . giving a child a credit card, not even bothering—"

"See, Dan?" my mother said. "Money isn't everything."

"Umm." I sat on the floor and faced the tree. What was all this about K.K. and B.J. and Felix and his father? The adults all knew, and apparently some kids at school knew, too. What was it? I wasn't going to find out now, that was for sure. One of these days, though, I'd ask Felix. He'd tell me if the time was right.

In the meantime—hey! What was I doing, sitting here? I rushed out to the kitchen to call Felix. My invitation would really bend his fenders!

17

◆ ◆ ◆

Our Silent One Speaks

On the day of Christmas Eve, Felix called to say he'd be over after dinner. He had to go out to eat with his dad.

That night we were sitting around listening to Mom bang out some carols on the piano. Grandpa said in a kidding way that she should have taken more lessons or maybe skipped them altogether. Mom just laughed.

A car pulled up, and I heard voices and then people coming up on the porch, stamping snow off their feet. I raced to the hall and flung the door open.

"Hi," Felix said. "Do you mind if B.J. comes in to see the tree and everything?"

I was really surprised to see her there. Grandma came to the doorway and invited B.J. in, and asked if whoever was in the car wanted to come in, too.

"No, it's just my father," Felix said. "He'll wait for B.J."

His father? What was he doing, hauling around Billie Jo?

B.J. kicked off her boots. She was wearing some sparkly kind of socks. In fact, almost everything she was wearing seemed to sparkle. I wasn't surprised to see that she'd even

118

put glittery gold makeup on her eyelids. She didn't just *do* anything if there was a way she could possibly *overdo* it.

B.J. eyed the tree. Then she took in the sprays of evergreen, the candles, the toy village. "Where are the stockings?" she asked me. "You do hang your sock up, don't you?"

I ignored the grin and said, "We'll do that later."

"You'd better go," Felix told her. "Dad's out there waiting."

B.J. turned. "You guys all have a cool yule," she said, and then she left. I thought I saw something orange flashing on her wrist.

"Martha," Dad said, "What are you doing?" My sister was sitting on the floor. She'd taken off her shoes and now she was yanking off a sock.

"She wants to hang it up," Grandma said. "Now, isn't that cute?"

"Sweetie, that's such a little sock," Grandpa said. "Don't you want to borrow one of my big ones?"

"Oh, Santa knows how to stretch them," Grandma said. "But you know, I just happen to have a special Christmas sock for you, dear. Now, let's see if I can find it."

"Come on, Felix, sit down," I said.

Grandma came back in a couple of minutes, holding a big red stocking with little toy designs woven into it. "This is for Martha," she said. I'd seen them at one of the stores that sold Christmas crafts.

"And here's one for Dan . . . and one for Felix."

What a gram! She must have gone out earlier that day

and gotten another one. Felix turned all pink, he was so pleased. "Wow," was all he could say.

We hooked the stockings over the fireplace, and then there was a little silence. That's when Martha did it. Spoke.

"When's Santa coming?" is what she said.

I could hear the intakes of breath from all the adults. And then squeals.

"Martha!" Mom grabbed her up. "You talked!" From Mom's excitement, you'd have thought my sister had done something spectacular, like spinning around on one toe while singing "The Star-Spangled Banner." "Did you hear that! My baby talked!"

Wouldn't you know that contrary sister of mine wouldn't say what I had coached her for several days now to say?

I looked at Felix, who had been in on the surprise. He shrugged and smiled. "At least she talked," he said.

I couldn't leave it at that. I went over to Martha and pulled away the arm she had around Mom's neck.

"What else can you say?" I asked her.

She looked at me as though I was some nut case.

"Say it, Martha."

She pulled her arm away and turned her face away, too.

"Give her to me, Mom."

Puzzled, Mom handed Martha over. I took her out to the hall. The adults were still thrilled beyond belief that this had happened—and on Christmas Eve!

"Listen, Martha," I said, putting her down and stooping to her level. "You go in there and say what you were going to say. Or Santa won't come tonight."

She stared at me, lips pursed. I knew she was trying to decide whether to cry or to punch me in the face.

"Martha, I mean it. Now, tell me what you're going to say." I put on my get-tough scowl. "Tell me, Martha."

She stuck out her lower lip, then grudgingly said, "Merry Christmas, everybody."

Then she did punch me, but I didn't care. "Go, Fido," I said, giving her a shove.

She marched back into the room. I followed. "Martha has something else to say. Say it, Martha."

She stamped her foot on mine, then said, "Merry Christmas, everybody. But not Dan."

That did actually blow everyone's doors off. In fact, it was too much, the way they were all laughing and carrying on. Martha kept on talking. Now she probably wouldn't shut up until she left for college.

I motioned for Felix to come along with me to the kitchen. "Let's load up on some food and drink and go upstairs," I said. "I've had enough of the miracle talker."

We took plates and piled them with fancy cookies and got cans of soda, two apiece.

"Is this the end of the festivities for tonight?" Felix wanted to know.

"Yeah. But we'll be up at the crack of dawn, ready or not."

"I'll be ready."

Quite a while later, Felix and I finished playing a game of chess and were just lolling around.

"How come B.J. was with you tonight?" I asked.

"Dad took us both out to dinner."

"How come?"

"He does that every once in a while. Sometimes we just eat at the house, though. We order in."

"I thought you considered B.J. pretty disgusting."

"I do."

"Then why do you spend time with her?"

"I don't have a lot of choice, Dan. She's just there sometimes. For meals or to stay all night. She has her own room."

"At *your* house?"

"Yeah."

"How come?"

"Because she's my half sister."

Speechless, I stared at Felix. Except for a flick of his eyes at me and away, Felix was expressionless.

After a few moments, I broke the silence with, "B.J.'s your half sister? But how can that be?"

Felix shrugged. "K.K. and my dad were once married."

"They were?" This was totally unexpected and unbelievable. Except that I had to believe it. "When?"

"Years ago. The marriage lasted about two minutes. They fought all the time. The combination was just too fiery. They still insult each other and yell sometimes when they meet."

"But B.J.?"

"Dad and K.K. split up before she was born. Then dad married my mom, and I came along."

"This just staggers me, Felix."

"I know. Pretty weird, huh?"

"Do the kids at school know . . . about you and B.J. being . . . it's hard to say . . . related?"

"I guess some know. Actually, no one really cares. But, Dan, there's a worse part. Something I guess I have to tell you."

"What?" *What now,* I wondered.

"Promise you won't feel mortified, being a friend and everything?"

"No. I mean I promise I won't be." *I hoped I wouldn't be.*

"Well . . . the truth is . . ." He swallowed. "I'm a grade ahead of myself."

"You're what?"

"I skipped third. I should be in fifth now. I'm . . ." he swallowed again . . . "Younger than B.J., even if we are in sixth grade together."

I stared at him. This was overwhelming news.

"I know," Felix said, looking down. "You feel revolted . . . being friends, hanging out with a kid younger than you. Can you understand why I hated to tell you? Do you want me to leave?"

"You idiot, I'm not revolted. I'm just amazed. I thought you were smart before, but now I see that you're brilliant."

"So, could we still hang around together? Not at school if it would embarrass you, but other times?"

"Hey, none of the stuff you told me matters. Well, it matters, I guess, but not as far as our being friends goes. Shake?"

We shook.

Felix gave a huge, satisfied sigh. "What a night. I'm glad

you found out about B.J. and everything. It's nauseating being in the same class with her. I pretend she's just another kid at school. She pretends the same thing."

We heard Mom coming up the stairs, talking to Martha. She knocked on my door, and both of them walked in.

"Better get to sleep, boys, before Santa comes," my mother said. "You know he won't leave any toys if you're awake."

"Oh, yeah," Felix said with a fake excitement. "What's he going to bring you, Martha?"

Martha stood with lips pressed together.

"Honey?" Mom said. "Tell Felix."

Martha glared. Then she said, "A tiger. To eat you up."

What a sweetheart. If I'd said that at her age, I'd have been scolded. But just the idea of Martha talking was so wonderful she could get away with saying *anything*. At least, until the novelty wore off.

18

♦ ♦ ♦ ─────────────────

Sleet and Ice Aren't So Nice

Christmas Day was everything Felix could have hoped for. It was traditional, from the getting up at dawn to see what Santa has brought to the big turkey dinner much later in the day. In between, neighbors and friends stopped by, and various members of the family played board games with Felix and me. Martha wouldn't let go of her monster even at nap time. My gifts were good, too, especially the electronic hockey game from SANTA, who seemed to have the same handwriting as my grandfather.

When Felix left, after thanking my folks and grandparents over and over, he told me this was the kind of perfect Christmas he had always imagined. I nodded, not saying, "Me, too." But that's what I was thinking.

It had started snowing on Christmas Day and continued the day after. On the morning of the sixth-grade sleepover, the sky was a dismal gray and there were a few snowflakes falling. They weren't the soft, fluffy kind. These were hard and gritty and stung when the wind whipped them at your face.

I had slept a little later than the adults, so I was sitting at the kitchen counter, eating cereal. Mom was filling a

vacuum bottle with coffee and putting together some turkey sandwiches.

"Rachel," Grandma said, "are you sure you want to
drive up north today? It looks really bad. I'm even wondering if your father and I should go out to the club for
luncheon and bridge."

"Oh, Mom."

Grandpa came in from the garage, rubbing his hands
together. "It's really cold out there," he said. "The wind
goes right through you."

"I was just saying," my grandmother remarked, "that I
didn't think it was a good day to drive up to see that cottage. It'll keep."

"Look," my mother said. "We've made up our minds.
We can't put this off for first one reason and then another."

"It's the night of the sleepover," I reminded Mom.

"As though I could forget," she said. "So what's the
problem?"

"Martha. Who's supposed to take care of her?"

"Oh, Dan. You can watch her until your grandparents
get back from playing bridge. Is that too much to ask?"

She didn't expect an answer.

So I got stuck baby-sitting, but it wasn't too bad. Martha was unusually quiet and even took a nap without my
threatening her or anything. In fact, I just found her on
the sofa, asleep.

I got about a million calls that afternoon, mostly from
Felix. B.J. rang me up to spread some gossip—none of the
parents could make it to the sleepover except Todd's

mother. Since she was the one who conked out no matter what, that was good news. Then I got some disturbing news. Grandpa called from the club, out somewhere in the rolling hills south of town, to say it had really snowed hard there and the snow had drifted over the lane. There was something wrong with the big snowplow, but as soon as they got it fixed and the lane cleared, everyone would be able to drive out.

"Just in case we're not home by the time you have to leave, take Martha along with you to the library," Grandpa said. "We'll pick her up there." And then he added, "It might be easier to pull her there on the sled than to try to get her to walk. How bad is it in town?"

"Not too bad."

"All right, we'll be there in a while."

They weren't, though. It was getting close to five o'clock, and there was no sign of them. I didn't have the number of the club. I didn't even know its name.

I got my stuff together—my pajamas, robe, slippers, sleeping bag. Then I looked outside. It was getting dark already. I waited until five thirty, and when there was still no sign of them I decided to get Martha ready. I knew very well that the minute I got her dressed and ready to go out, my grandparents would pull up.

They didn't, though.

Martha was whiny. She wanted her mommy. Well, so did I. Why did our parents have to take off on one of the most important days and nights of my life?

"Martha, we're going to the library," I said. "B.J. is going to be there. You like her, don't you? You should.

She's as hard to get along with as you are." When Martha scowled, I said, "I meant that as a compliment."

I was shoving her into her snowsuit. There was no use in changing her clothes or anything, because I was sure that just as soon as we got to the library my grandparents would come along.

Martha scrunched up her toes when I was trying to tug on her boots. She made fists of her hands when I put on her mittens. I thought for about the thousandth time that when I grew up I was not going to get married and have any kids. They could be easygoing and fun to be with, like me, but there was always that outside chance of another Martha showing up. It was just too big a risk.

I got her outside finally, and onto the sled. I put my supplies on the sled behind her and tied them so that she couldn't shove them into a snowbank along the way.

It was really tough going. The wind was pushing against me, and I had to lean forward, keeping my head down, because of the snow. It was a hard, driving snow that stung my cheeks. Martha was protected a little by my body, but even so I stopped and pulled her knitted cap and hood down as far as they would go.

Cars were moving slowly along the streets, and once in a while one would hit a slick spot and go into a skid. I began worrying about my grandparents driving and, more than that, about my parents. I just hoped they had got to where they were going before now.

There was a traffic tangle in front of the library, with cars driving up and letting kids off, snow swirling in front of the headlights. One car had its left front wheel stuck in a snowdrift and was racing its engine. Kids in bunches were coming along the sidewalks, struggling against the wind, arms loaded with stuff.

I got to the front doors of the library, hauled Martha off the sled, got my gear, and put the sled just inside the door, leaning it against the wall. Along with everyone else, I pulled off my boots, and then Martha's, and just left them out in the hall.

Kids' faces were red from the wind, and there was enough nose sniffling to drown out the sound of a fire alarm. Everyone was in a good mood, though. Even Mrs. Gayle, standing in the doorway leading to the main room, seemed cheerful. I wondered if she got overtime for the sleepover.

"I had to bring the pest along for a while," I told her, "until my grandparents pick her up." Before Mrs. Gayle could even answer, Amanda and B.J. hauled Martha away. I turned to Felix. "Why do they think Martha's so adorable? Are girls like that, or what?"

"They're like that," Felix said. "Or else it may be their way of playing up to you."

"What?"

"Come on, Dan. You must have noticed by now that Amanda likes you and B.J. is kind of nuts about you. Although, of course, B.J. is kind of nuts, period. Want to go stake out a spot?"

I followed him in a daze. Did Amanda like me? And if so, how much? There's *like*, as in *I like movies,* and then there's *like* as in *really like.* Which was it with Amanda?

"Looks like there's no room next to Traci and Shirley,"

Felix said. "Let's just camp over here. Where'd you put your sack dinner?"

I felt sunken. "I forgot." Would I have time to dash home for it? Or rather, push my way back through the heavy weather?

"Hey, not to worry," Felix said. "I have plenty."

"Everyone!" It was Mrs. Gayle, hands to her mouth, megaphone style. "Those of you who brought flashlights, check them up here."

"My folks made me bring one," Susan somebody called out.

"That's all right. Some of you needed them on the way over, but you won't need them tonight, so just get them up here."

Felix and I strolled toward the other kids. It looked as though everyone was here already, including Todd's mom. She was a big woman, wearing jeans and a sweatshirt that said, *Have a Good Day Somewhere Else.*

"Hey, Mrs. Barry," Felix said in a good-natured way, "it's nice to see you here."

She looked up from a newspaper. "Yeah, well, I'd rather be off stomping grapes or herding goats, but I figure this is the next best thing." She went back to her newspaper, which was one of those sleaze things you can buy in a supermarket.

"What is she," I whispered to Felix, "a stand-up comedian? Or in her case, a sit-down?"

"She's a fall-asleeper, that's all that matters here," Felix said.

There was a lot of commotion and talking and yelling back and forth, but through it all I thought I heard Martha. Sure enough, when I went to the children's room, she was in there whining, while the girls were kneeling in front of her, trying to coax her into a better mood.

Amanda looked up and saw me. "She wants to take the rabbits out of the cages," she said. "I know it's not allowed."

As she was saying the words, Martha pulled away from her, toddled to the snake cage, and grabbed at the latch.

"Martha, stop that!" I shouted. She started yelling.

I went over, yanked her around to face me, and said, "If you don't stop that right now . . ." I didn't know what to say, here in front of the girls.

"You will *what?*" she said. Why did I ever wish this kid would start to talk? She stuck out her lower lip in the look I knew so well.

B.J. saved me by saying, "If you let out the snake, it'll spit poison into the air and we'll all disintegrate, poof." She snapped her fingers. "Like that!"

"Billie Jo," Amanda objected, "you're going to scare the poor little thing."

"Oh, get real," B.J. said. "This kid doesn't scare. She's not even afraid of these snakes. Anyway, they're totally harmless." B.J. reached to unlatch the cage.

"No! Don't you dare!" Amanda said, backing away and pulling Martha with her. "They ought to keep them locked up. In fact, they shouldn't even have stuff like that in here, with little children around."

"Amanda, you're such a wet noodle." B.J. lifted out a snake and held it in the middle so both ends wiggled. "See, it's like a toy."

I took Martha's hand, and just before she yanked it away I thought that it felt a little hot. I hoped she hadn't gotten frostbite on the way over, but she hadn't complained. She let Amanda take her hand, and I stayed behind to make sure B.J. put the snake back into the cage. I didn't trust her any farther than I could throw a piano. And I certainly didn't blame Felix for acting like they weren't related. I'd hate to have B.J. in my family.

There weren't quite as many kids in the main part of the library as before. The younger ones who'd been there after school were being picked up by parents, and even some of the sixth-graders seemed to be missing.

"Where is everybody?" I asked. And then I saw through the big picture windows that there were bunches of kids out skating on the lake. "Isn't that dangerous?" I asked Felix. "Couldn't they . . . like . . . fall through the ice?"

"Are you kidding?" We saw B.J., all bundled up and with skates slung over her shoulder, head for the back door. "That ice is so thick by now you could drive a car over it."

I stared at Felix. Was he putting me on?

"No kidding. People drive Jeeps over the ice for short-cuts during the winter, and there are snowmobiles on the lake all the time. I'd be out there now, too, but who wants to skate in weather like this? I think those guys are crazy."

Some of them began heading back indoors. They said

the wind was too strong, and besides it was starting to sleet.

Mrs. Gayle was walking around, giving instructions, and even Todd's mother was up on her feet. They were getting the kids to unroll their sleeping bags to save their places, and then telling them to wash up and get ready to eat.

Amanda came over with Martha. "I hope she likes pizza," she said.

"She's crazy about it. But she won't be here by nine o'clock, when they deliver."

"There's been a change in plans," Amanda said. "The pizza place called and they're going to deliver right away. They said they may not be able to drive later, with the ice storm on the way."

"Ice storm?" Just the words chilled me. "What . . . what is that like?"

"Oh, it's awful. It would cut your face just to be out in it, and the trees get coated and branches break off. And you don't dare drive. Cars spin out of control because the roads are like sheets of glass. It's really awful."

The vision of my parents spinning around on icy roads flashed through my mind. Would they drive in weather like that? Yes, if my mother wanted to. Why couldn't she be a limp wimp instead of always bossing the whole family around? But maybe this time my dad would take charge and say they weren't going to drive. He might.

And how about my grandparents? Were they on their way? Twice, the front door opened, but it was only parents who'd come to pick up their kids because of the coming storm. The kids—Tish and Alyssa—put up a howl, but their folks said it wasn't safe for them to be away from home on a night like this.

B.J. walked in from the back. Her face was so red, you could hardly see the freckles. "I'm the last one to give up on the skating," she said. "It's not a fit night for man or beast."

"You're not a man, B.J.," someone yelled, "so you must be a—"

"Cram it," B.J. said.

Amanda was just bringing Martha back from the washroom when the pizza man arrived. A shout went up, and there was a wild scramble for places at the library tables. Amanda and I sat with Martha between us. Felix sat next to me. Mrs. Gayle passed out paper plates and napkins, and Todd's mom handed sodas around. Then they put the pizzas in the middle of the tables, with about four kids to each pizza.

As hands grabbed, Todd's mom called out, "Now don't act like pigs around a trough, show some class." She shook her head as everyone continued grabbing and stuffing their faces.

I handed a small slice to Martha. She just sat there with her stubborn look. Over her head, I motioned for Amanda to get Martha to eat. She tried, but Martha still wouldn't.

"I guess she's shy," Amanda said.

"Yeah," I told her. "Shy like a rattlesnake." I shouldn't have said that, but I just wasn't used to being around sweet girls like Amanda. Then I whispered, "Don't pay any attention to her. She'll eat it." Martha looked up and scowled.

I really didn't enjoy the food, what with Martha just sitting there and Amanda giving me worried looks. I didn't understand it. Never had I seen my sister refuse pizza. And there was no question of her being shy. Not Martha. Was she sick?

I leaned down and put my hand on her forehead. It was hot.

"Martha, are you okay?" I asked.

For reply, she flung my hand away. She was okay.

After we'd finished eating and had tossed all the garbage into big trash cans, we went to our own spots and sat there for story time. This was a read-aloud, with Mrs. Gayle starting and then calling on various kids to come read a few pages. She'd picked a spooky story. It got scarier and scarier, until I could almost imagine a chill running down my spine.

Then I did feel a chill. A really cold chill. That was when the lights went out. All the lights . . . leaving us in total darkness.

19

Snake Hunt
at the Sleepover

For a few seconds, there was only the sound of howling winds and creaking trees. Then everyone started cheering.

"Quiet!" Mrs. Gayle yelled. "Don't get your hopes up. The lights will come back on—"

"Sure they will," Felix said. "In about a week."

"Really . . . a week?" I hoped Felix couldn't hear the tremble in my voice.

Mrs. Gayle was shouting again. "Fortunately, we have a few flashlights. Now, just stay put. We don't want anyone stumbling around and getting hurt."

It was pitch-black in the library, with even the streetlights out. Then a beam of light appeared, and I could see Mrs. Gayle at least.

"You people who brought flashlights may come up and get them," she said. "The rest of you stay where you are."

I was wondering if I should go find Martha. She was still with the girls on the other side of the room. Oh, well, why look for trouble?

"Dan . . . ." Felix said in an undertone. I could hardly

hear him through the noise and confusion. "Don't worry about a thing. I brought a superpowered flashlight that'll send a beam for miles."

"Good," I said. I actually didn't know why that was so wonderful. Was it my imagination, or was the room getting cold?

"Quiet, please!" Mrs. Gayle was yelling.

"Hey! All you hound dogs!" That was Todd's mom's voice. "Shut up and quiet down or I'll pitch you out on your ears!"

"What a sweetheart," Felix murmured. "Shouldn't she be asleep by now?"

Eventually everyone quieted down. Mrs. Gayle, after telling everyone else to keep their flashlights off "to conserve the batteries," she said, used hers to keep on reading.

It was definitely getting chillier in the room. I wasn't the only one to notice; I could hear kids softly complaining. Finally, someone must have mentioned it to Mrs. Gayle.

"People," she said, "the heat in this building is electric, so of course it's gone off, too. I suggest you keep on your regular clothes but get into your sleeping bags."

She waited out the scrambling and yakking that followed.

"Maybe I'd better go get Martha," I said to Felix. "If I can find my way over . . ."

"Why don't you leave well enough alone?" he answered. "B.J. and Amanda seem to be able to handle her all right."

That was fine by me.

With her flashlight pointed at the book, Mrs. Gayle

picked up where she'd left off. Her face looked eerie in the reflected light.

I was pretty sure that when she'd chosen that story to read, she'd had no idea how spooky it would be to hear it in almost total darkness. For a second it occurred to me that she'd had someone turn off the power deliberately, just for effect, but that was crazy. She'd never do that. Besides, the streetlights were out, and even houses down the street were completely dark.

"*When suddenly, something soft and squishy,*" she read, "*brushed against my arm.*"

A girl yelled. There was a general buzzing of words, like "You're such a sissy," plus others more crude. Then the girl, whoever she was, shouted, "I don't care! I did feel something!"

"Now folks, if you're going to keep interrupting, we can just forget . . ." Mrs. Gayle sounded a little stressed out. The kids, of course, advised each other to gag themselves, and the story continued. It went on for maybe ten minutes and then there was an all-out scream.

"I don't care! I don't care! I felt it, I'm telling you! Give me that light!" Someone did, and then the girl screamed louder than ever.

Mrs. Gayle had by then made her way over through the tangle of sleeping bags, flashlight in hand.

"I don't see anything," she said. "Now, Darlene . . ."

And then there was another scream, this time behind her. We'd all crept closer by now.

"There, there!"

Mrs. Gayle flashed the light around, just in time to see

a tail disappear under a sleeping bag to the tune of several more screams. The girls, and the guys, too, were out of their sleeping bags by now, hopping around, yelling in fear, or just for the fun of it.

"Oh, for cripe's sake," B.J. said, crawling up to the scene. "It's only a little garter snake, nothing to be scared about."

"Snake! Snake!" From the panic, you'd have thought it was Godzilla himself, showing up in full color.

B.J. made things even worse by grabbing one and swinging it around. "See? Just a slimy little snake!"

"How'd they get out?" someone asked.

"They? There are more?" Kids climbed up on the library tables, even the checkout desk. I didn't, though I admit it seemed like a pretty good idea.

"Keep calm," Mrs. Gayle shouted. "I'll go see if any others got out. B.J., bring that snake along."

The kids with flashlights were waving them around, looking for other escapees. I could dimly see Amanda. I went over and sat on the edge of the table next to her. She cuddled up close to me, and I put my arm around her. It was okay, wasn't it? I was just protecting her. Wow.

"I hope the poor baby isn't scared," Amanda whispered. Did she mean me?

"Where *is* Martha?" Amanda asked.

Martha. I had forgotten about Martha. "I thought she was with you."

"I thought she was with *you.*"

Where was Martha? Oh-oh. *That's* where she was, I bet. "I'd better go look."

"I'll come along," Amanda said.

Felix came with us, too, and when we reached the children's room he flashed his light around. We saw what I thought we'd see. My sister. She was standing, her hands behind her, with that typical lower-lip-stuck-out look of hers. The flashlight beam now picked out the animal cages. Every door was open.

Mrs. Gayle took a quick count. "I hate to say this," she told us, "but there are three rabbits, five gerbils, and two snakes missing."

Other kids, several of them with lights, had streamed into the room by now. They started scrambling around as though this was a live-action treasure hunt.

A guy yelled, "There's a snake wrapped around my leg!" but it was just some kid grabbing his ankle.

"No hysteria, please!" Mrs. Gayle shouted. "Would you just go back and try to calm down? You're frightening the poor animals."

It did no good. Lights were flashing everywhere—on the floor, walls, and ceiling.

"Keep the lights down so we can see where we're stepping," a kid yelled out. "I don't want to squash the guts out of a gerbil."

"I found one," Linda called out. "A gerbil. Behind the wastebasket."

Eventually all the lost animals were located.

"Now, please," Mrs. Gayle said, "the safari's over. You big-game hunters can head back to camp." The kids left the room, many of them making wild-animal sounds.

Felix, who seemed to have forgotten his plan to protect

Traci and Shirley, stayed behind to light our way. I knelt down by my sister. "Why'd you do that, Martha?" I asked. "You know, we told you—"

She started to cry.

"Hey, it's over, don't cry." That's all we needed, the kid working herself up to a major howl.

It wasn't like Martha to fling her arms around my neck. It wasn't like Martha to feel so . . . so burning up, either. Her cheeks against mine were like hot coals.

"Martha, are you sick?" I asked.

She cried harder. "I want Mommy."

"Mommy . . . Mommy will be here soon," I lied. Were they home yet? I wondered. And what about my grandparents?

I carried Martha out to the front desk. "I've got to call home," I told Mrs. Gayle.

"You can't, Dan. The phones aren't working."

"Maybe they're fixed by now," I said. I picked up the phone. It was dead.

"The crews are probably out working right now," Mrs. Gayle said in a hopeful way. "It won't be long . . ."

Martha struggled toward Amanda. Amanda took her. After a few minutes she asked for me again.

"Why don't we all move our stuff together?" B.J. suggested. "To keep Martha happy?"

So, to keep Martha happy, we did. Amanda and B.J. got some kids to move so they could be right in front of Felix and me. Martha kept going from one to the other. She whimpered a lot.

A boy named Joe volunteered to read. It wasn't a great

success because some of the kids would give fake screams over the slightest little incident. A few jokers started snoring.

Mrs. Gayle moved over to us. "How's your sister?" she whispered.

"She's dozing a little," I said.

"Good."

"But she feels like she's burning up," I added.

Mrs. Gayle touched her forehead. "Oh, dear," she said. "She must have a very high fever. I have children's aspirin, but I'm not allowed to give it without permission. If only . . ."

. . . *The electricity, or even the phones, would come back on,* I thought.

"Well, we can only wait. . . ." the librarian said doubtfully, and moved over to where some kids were punching each other back and forth.

Wait, I thought. That was the hardest thing she could ask me to do.

20

A Thrilling Lights-and-Siren Rescue

According to Felix's watch, it was now close to nine o'clock. Joe's story finally ended.

"I'm hungry," someone said, and others took up the complaint.

Mrs. Gayle said they could eat the food they'd brought from home. "Those with flashlights can set them up so we can all see what we're doing," she said.

"I brought treats for everyone," Connie called out. "Twinkies!"

"How appropriate," B.J. muttered. "Anyone want a sardine and peanut butter sandwich?"

"Not unless you have chopped liver on the side," Felix said cheerfully. "Here, Dan, try a ham and cheese if that's not too boring."

"I'm not really hungry," I said. I was holding Martha, who was half asleep but still whimpering now and then. It scared me, the way she seemed to be burning up. I felt so helpless.

"Poor baby . . ." Amanda hovered over Martha and

then reached to brush a curl damp with sweat away from her cheek. She turned worried eyes toward me. "Dan . . ."

"I know." My voice quivered. "I don't know what to do."

B.J. had crawled up. "What's the matter?"

"Martha's really sick. She has a fever."

"Maybe it's an appendicitis attack," B.J. said. "That's what a neighbor kid had . . . and they had to rush him—"

Martha put a hand against an ear and cried.

Her ear? Oh, no, not that. "She had a terrific ear infection about a year ago," I said, now more worried than ever.

"Oh, that's bad," B.J. said. "I wouldn't be surprised if her eardrum burst. That happened to a girl my cousin knows."

"B.J., would you please just shut up?" Felix said. "Look, guys, we've got to do something for this kid. But what?"

"Maybe I should try to get home to see if there's any ear medicine left from last time," I said.

Martha cried and clung to me all the tighter.

"Someone's got to get a doctor," B.J. said. "And I know just where to find one."

"Where?" we all asked.

"There's a hospital right across the lake—back in that direction."

"Brilliant, B.J.," Felix said. "We all know that."

"Yeah? What you don't know is how to get there. I do."

"You do?"

B.J. glanced around to make sure no adult was within earshot. "Sure. On skates."

"You can't get there on skates," Felix said. "It's got to be a mile, or almost."

"I'll do it." B.J. scooted away from her sleeping bag.

"No," Felix said, "I'll do it."

"Oh, give yourself a break," B.J. said. "You're out of shape. The only part of you that gets a daily workout is your typing fingers."

"I can't let you do that, B.J.," I said. "It's freezing out there. You could . . ." I was going to say *fall through the ice*, but I guessed she was lighter than a Jeep. "You could . . . freeze."

"Let me be the one to worry about that," B.J. said. She scooted backward a little. Then she scooted up again to whisper, "Now don't tell anyone, especially Mrs. G. She'd freak out. I'll just sneak into the hall and grab my stuff and then get going."

"You want my flashlight?" Felix asked.

"What do you think I am, some kind of fool? I brought my own, plus extra batteries." She disappeared in the shadows.

I had to admit a feeling of admiration for B.J. She thought of everything. I felt useless by comparison.

Martha started crying again, harder. She flung her hands to her ears and cheeks but also bent almost double. Maybe she did have appendicitis. Plus the earache.

Mrs. Gayle came over. "Dan, I don't care about the rule. I've brought the baby aspirin and water. Will she take it for you?"

"I'll try." But Martha fought off the pills.

Mrs. Gayle's voice was quite concerned. "Maybe I should try to drive somewhere for help."

"Oh, don't do that, Mrs. Gayle," Amanda said. "I have a feeling that help is on the way."

"I have the same feeling," I said.

"Well . . . let's hope you're both right." The librarian put a reassuring hand on my shoulder, then walked away.

"Don't worry, Dan," Amanda breathed softly. "B.J.'s weird, but you can count on her in a crisis."

However, I *was* worried. How long would it take B.J. to make it across the lake? Could she make it at all? The thought of B.J. falling, maybe breaking a leg, freezing, made me stiffen. Wasn't there *something* I could do? Maybe I could take Felix's flashlight and . . . and what? Walk the long way to the hospital? It would take forever.

I turned. "Felix, do you think . . ." Felix wasn't there.

Maybe he'd gone to the washroom. Kids were going back and forth all the time. I'd go see, but I couldn't unclench Martha from my arm.

"Frank," I called out to a kid just coming back, "is Felix in the washroom?"

"How should I know? I didn't take the roll."

"Well, just go look, Frank!" Amanda said in a no-nonsense tone. The kid did and reported Felix wasn't there.

"Ohhh," Amanda whispered. "He's gone after B.J. I know it."

Was that bad or good? If Felix saved B.J. from disaster, that was positive. If he got hurt himself, negative.

"Amanda, I don't know what to do," I said.

"Ssssh. You're doing what you have to do . . . looking after your baby sister. I think you're really sweet, Dan."

For a moment my cheeks felt as warm as Martha's. But I filed Amanda's words away for a future time when I wouldn't be so worried.

Minutes dragged into what seemed like hours. Slowly, it became more silent in the room as kids fell asleep. The ones still awake whispered to one another. I put Martha down, and although she whimpered she didn't wake up. I started crawling toward the back window and Amanda followed. When we got there, I breathed on the lower pane and rubbed the frost that was beginning to form.

"Look over there, far out on the lake," I whispered. "Flickering lights. Think that's B.J. and Felix?"

"I hope." Amanda pointed beyond. "See that band of light? It must be the hospital."

"How would they have lights?"

"Hospitals have generators in case of emergencies." She was so smart.

Just then the lights flashed on in the library, but before we could cheer, they went off again. This happened a couple of times.

"They'll come on and stay on in a while," Mrs. Gayle announced. "The crews are working."

I wished they'd work faster. Another half hour passed. I felt stiff from the cold and tension. Martha was still waking and dozing and whimpering. Where were Mom and Dad? Where was B.J.? Felix? Grandpa and Grandma? Were they all frozen?

Just when I was feeling almost sick from worry, too

scared even to talk anymore, I saw some flashing lights reflected on the ceiling. They were red and white.

"Hey!" someone yelled. "There's an ambulance out there!"

"Ambulance!" The kids who were awake stumbled toward the front window. The sleepers stirred and asked what was going on.

"It *is* an ambulance!" a kid shouted, and someone else said, "You ignorant slug, it's the paramedics!"

I didn't care what it was, so long as it was help.

The knock on the front door had hardly sounded when it was yanked open by somebody. And at that moment, when the paramedics walked in, the lights came on and stayed on!

"All right, where's the sick child?" one of the guys called out. And to my great, great relief, B.J. bombed along in front of him and pointed in my direction. And there was Felix, too, looking pink-cheeked and proud.

I got up and held out Martha to the ambulance man, who turned out to be a genuine doctor from the hospital. Martha started crying harder.

"Is there some room where we can go?" the doctor asked Mrs. Gayle. She led him to the little office behind the desk. I started to follow, but Mrs. Gayle said, "Dan, you'd better wait."

I turned to see kids clustered around B.J. Her face was fiery red, but she was smiling bigger than those *Have a good day!* stickers.

"B.J.!" I shouted. "You made it!"

"Of course," she said, with no trace of modesty. "How could you even doubt it?"

"We were so scared for you," Amanda said. "Weren't we, Dan?"

"Scared to death," I said. "Not that we doubted you, of course. But it was so cold out there . . . and so dark. . . ."

"Well," B.J. said, "I have to admit that Felix's flashlight was a big help. It beamed me across. And then when he switched to the SOS signals, the hospital picked them up and was on the alert. In fact, the paramedics were right at the edge of the lake when I came staggering up. So it was really Felix—"

"No, Sis, it was both of us."

The impact of what he'd said—calling B.J. Sis for probably the first time—hit us all. As for B.J., her eyes widened and she tried to shrug, but she couldn't stop the pleased look from spreading all over her face.

Someone broke the spell with, "I wonder if the phones are working." They were. At first kids wanted to call home, but thinking it over, they decided not to. They might have to leave.

I tried calling my grandparents. There was no answer.

"Here comes someone in a Jeep!" a kid shouted. "I hope it's not the school principal!"

"Not unless he's bringing more pizza!"

It was my grandparents, with their neighbor who owned the Jeep.

"Dan! We just got back, just a few minutes ago!" Grandma said breathlessly. "Harold . . . Mr. Wellington was running the engine of his Jeep to keep it from freezing, and he offered to bring us over. We thought we could take Martha home so the whole night wouldn't be spoiled for you."

Grandpa interrupted Grandma with, "Dan, where *is* Martha? You didn't leave her—!" He looked a bit shocked. He looked even more shocked when I told him Martha was in with the doctor.

"Doctor!" they both shouted at once. "Martha's sick?"

"It may be her ear again," I said. "Or maybe appendicitis."

"What!" Grandma practically shrieked.

"It's probably not both," I said, trying to calm her.

"Where's that baby?" Grandma shoved Grandpa's hand away from her shoulder. "I'm going to that baby—"

Just then the doctor came out, holding Martha. My grandparents rushed toward him. We all did.

"Don't tell me, doctor, that you have to operate!" my grandmother cried, reaching for and taking Martha. "Such a little thing. . . ." She felt her head. "Poor baby, she's got a fever . . . but *operate?* Isn't there something . . . ?"

The doctor smiled. "Operate? Ma'am, are you the child's—"

"I'm her grandmother. Before you do anything drastic, don't you think you should . . . I don't know . . . get a second opinion?"

The doctor smiled more. "I really don't think that's necessary. The symptoms are pretty clear. This child is coming down with chicken pox."

Chicken pox. Why couldn't I have figured that one out? Or Felix? Or B.J.? I guess none of us was thinking straight.

Life with Martha, I could see, would always have its surprises.

21

Surprising Change of Plans

It was too cold for Martha to ride home in the Jeep, so the paramedics said they'd drive her and Grandma in the ambulance.

"How about you, Dan?" Grandma asked. "Do you want to come along?"

I didn't know. In a way, I wanted to finish off what was left of the sleepover, but then again, I thought I ought to go with Martha.

"Are you going to run the lights and siren?" Felix asked the guy.

"If the folks want 'em, they've got 'em."

"Go," Felix said to me.

I grabbed my stuff, said good-bye to Amanda, Felix, B.J., and everyone, and left with cheers sounding in my ears. *"Dan, Dan, he's our man!"* the kids were yelling. I didn't know why, but it was great.

"My goodness, you're popular," Grandma said as we braved the wind outside. She was carrying Martha, wrapped in a blanket from the ambulance.

"I guess they liked the excitement we provided. They ought to be cheering the rescue team, Felix and B.J."

"I want to hear more about that later," Grandma said.

*

When we got back home, the phone was ringing, and I snatched it up.

It was my mother. "Where *were* you?" she began. "I've been calling for at least an hour!"

"Where are *you*?" I shot back. "We were scared stiff about you. Just now, in the ambulance, Grandma was saying—"

"*Ambulance!* My God, what's happened? Someone's had a heart attack! My father . . . was he shoveling snow in all this weather?"

"No, it wasn't anything like that, Mom. It was just Martha."

"Martha! Oh, no! What was it? Don't tell me! Oh, I can't stand it. Here's your father—"

"What is it?" he cried out. "What's with Martha?"

"Nothing."

"Nothing! You told your mother—"

"Dad, she just has chicken pox."

"Chicken pox? Then why the ambulance?"

"It's a long story, Dad."

"Well, tell it short. No, let me speak to one of your grandparents. Where's Martha now?"

"In bed. Here's Grandpa."

I was glad it was my grandfather who'd come into the room. Briefly, he told my parents what had happened and found out they'd be back in the morning. My grandmother would have had more to say. It seems to be the women in our family who speak their minds. And it looked like Martha was going to be right up there with them.

•

My parents showed up at around noon the next day, with Mom crying out, "Where's my baby?"

"Asleep. She's fine, just let her be," Grandma said.

My dad came in after stomping his feet on the doorstep. "Wow," he said, "is it ever good to be back! What an experience."

After they'd checked on Martha, we all sat around the dining room table drinking coffee and hot chocolate. My mother looked a bit pale, and my father seemed really beat.

"It was snow and ice all the way," he said. "We could hardly see the road, and because of new snow, we couldn't see the ice patches, either. We almost plowed into a truck one time."

My grandmother gave a little gasp.

"Did you get to where you wanted to go?" my grandfather asked.

"No way. We stopped for gas, and the guy said it was even worse ahead. He told us no one in his right mind would even think of going to that resort. He said it was deserted at this time of year. There was no motel, not even a grocery store open."

I remembered that was exactly what B.J.'s mother had told Mom.

My mother broke in. "That's why we decided to turn

around and come back, but the snow got so heavy we had to give up. There were cars in ditches and emergency vehicles all over the place. You've no idea how awful it was."

My grandmother cleared her voice.

Oh-oh, I thought. *Here it comes.*

"Now listen to me, you two," she said. "I don't care what your thoughts are about living with nature, close to the soil and all that rubbish. You have a responsibility to two children, who do not need to be dragged up to some forsaken wilderness to live off berries and roots."

"But, Mother—"

"Just a minute, I'm not finished," Grandma continued. "Imagine if you'd been living up in that place and the baby did come down with appendicitis, or if Dan here fell and broke his leg—"

"Mother—" Mom said.

"No, Rachel, I just won't allow it. You're the mother, but I'm the grandmother, and I'm telling you—"

"I'm trying to tell you something. We've changed our minds."

"I don't care . . . what? What did you say?" Grandma asked.

"I said we don't want to move up there anymore."

"You don't?" My grandparents looked taken aback. As for me, I guess *stunned* would be the word.

"We changed our minds," Dad said.

There was a silence as his words really sank in. Then my grandfather asked, "Was it the weather that made you change?"

"That clinched it, but even before . . ." Dad began.

Mom looked down, and then with an apologetic little smile said, "All right, let's be honest. I'd begun having second thoughts a while back, but I just wouldn't give in to them. You know how stubborn—"

"You?" Grandma said with a smile. "Stubborn?"

"Okay, okay." Mom held up her hands in an I-surrender way.

Dad put an arm around her shoulders. "It's true. Rachel told me that lately she was having doubts, but I thought we ought to go up and be sure. Well, now, after this near disaster we're double sure, aren't we, hon?"

Mom nodded. "I think I'm finally ready to settle down in some sensible place." She looked at me. "What do you think, Danny?"

"Sure." *What was her idea of a sensible place?*

"What place did you have in mind?" my grandmother asked. She looked braced for any answer. And so was I.

My dad, trying to hold back a smile, said, "I know we're a big burden, but could we hang around here?"

"Here?" Grandma asked. "Here with us?" She sounded so pleased.

"Just a while longer," Mom said. "Until we can find a place of our own here in town."

My grandparents were smiling as if they'd won the lottery. "You know you can stay in this house as long as you like," Grandma said. "We certainly have room to spare."

"Well, we'll be out before the tourist season," my father assured her.

"Oh, the tourists can go somewhere else," Grandma

said. "Come here, Dan, and give me a hug." I did, and Grandma gave me a big hug back.

So just like that it was settled. The thing that had upset me for months . . . gone. That's where adults have it all over kids. They can decide. Kids just have to go along. But if I ever have any kids of my own, I'll let them help with the deciding. I mean it.

I rushed to the phone and called Felix. He told B.J., and from then on it might as well have been on the five o'clock news.

Kids started calling me. "Glad you'll be staying here," was what most of them said. Troy even said it was smart of me to have trained Martha that way.

"What way?" I asked.

"You know, to go let the animals out at just the right time . . . when the library was dark and scary."

"Troy, that wasn't my idea."

"Get outta here! A little kid like that couldn't do it on her own. You're just being modest."

"Oh, well," I said, letting it go and wondering what new tricks my sister would pull when she really hit her stride.

Joe and a couple of others went on about the kind of excitement I'd provided . . . paramedics, ambulances, sirens. "It was a lot better than last year with that stupid cardboard skeleton," Joe said.

Again, I tried not to take credit. "It was Billie Jo and Felix who brought help," I said.

"Yes, but you brought Martha, who was the cause of it all."

Amazing. The one thing I thought they'd sneer about—hauling in my baby sister—had made me some kind of hero.

I talked to Felix about it when I went over to his house the next day. "Don't get me wrong," I told him. "I'm glad that the kids suddenly think I'm great stuff, but I didn't do a thing."

"Don't fight it," he advised. "If they want to think you even engineered the sleet storm, let them." He gave me a little punch on the arm. "Boy, it was a lot better than last year's sleepover."

"That's what they all say."

Felix's phone rang and he answered. "Yes, he's here," he said. He handed the phone to me, making a revolting smacking sound.

It was Amanda.

"I just wondered how Martha is," she said. "Your mother said you were over at Felix's house."

She could have asked my mother how Martha was, couldn't she? "Martha's fine," I said. "Whiny but not really sick." I turned my back to Felix, who was rolling his eyes and pursing his lips. "How are you?" *Don't tell me you've got the chicken pox!*

"I'm okay. Dan, do you still want to help with the Snowfest?"

"Sure."

"Then could we get together . . . maybe at the library . . . this afternoon?"

"Sounds good." I moved away from Felix, who was trying to listen in. "What time?"

"About two."

"Okay, I'll see you. So long."

"So long, sweetie!" Felix said in a high-pitched voice as I hung up the phone.

"You chocolate-covered French fried banana!" I said, giving him a fake punch on the arm like the one he'd given me.

Felix sank slowly to the floor. Then he got up, wriggling and twisting and singing some stupid banana song with a Spanish accent. I think it was from an old TV commercial.

I just stood there, shaking my head. It's hard to figure how someone so totally nuts can also be so totally brilliant. I guess Felix is a freak of nature. I'm really lucky to have him for a friend.

22

Just a Born Genius

F elix walked to the library with me, a little early. Mrs. Gayle waved us over to her desk.

"I hear," she said to me, "that your folks have decided to stay in town. Dottie Hanson from the gallery told me. She's thrilled that a well-known artist like your mother will be showing her new work here."

"Your mom will probably clean up in this town," Felix said to me. "Rake it in."

"It'll be wonderful, too, to have a dedicated woman like her on our environmental-protection committee," Mrs. Gayle said. "And your father, too. Will he teach here, do you know?"

"Yeah, he's already substitute teaching," I said. She nodded. "And there's a college job coming up that I think he'll try to get now."

"Mrs. Gayle," Felix said, "I wonder if you've made any plans."

"At the library we're always full of plans," she said. "Did you have something special in mind?"

"As a matter of fact, yes. What about next year's sleep-over?"

"Next year's sleepover?" Mrs. Gayle closed her eyes, put both palms on the checkout counter, and lowered her head. Then she slowly raised it and said, "Child, do you know what you're asking? It's been how many days?"

Felix patted her hand. "There, there."

"My head is beginning to clear, but the muscles are still shrieking and my nerves—"

"Take two aspirins and call me in the morning." Felix patted Mrs. Gayle's hand again. "Come, Dan."

We started to walk away.

"Boys," she called. We stopped and turned.

"What do you think we should have next year? Pizza again, or tacos?"

"Both!" someone shouted.

It was B.J., walking in with Amanda. She swept up to the desk. The rest of us grouped around her.

"I've been doing some thinking," Billie Jo said. Ignoring Felix's groan, she went on, "So far the sleepover has had a spooky episode and a stirring rescue adventure." She dipped her knee in a mock curtsy. "Next year we should try to top all that."

"And you know how," Mrs. Gayle said in an interested but wary voice.

"Naturally. We'll have a talent show. And I'll be the star attraction, with a song and tap routine I'm working on right now."

"B.J.," Felix said, "give the world a break. Turn to science, go into orbit for a million years."

"Oh, Felix, be nice," Amanda said. "Talent is rare. A

person who has it ought to share it." She turned and gave me a look that seemed to say, *I'm really talking about you and art.*

We laughed and went over to sit at a library table. "Now, for the Snowfest. . . ." Amanda pulled papers out of a plaid folder. "What do you think?"

All I could think was how good it felt to be here, among friends, and to get to stay. But I said, "How about some giant snow cones . . . with colored tops, reflector lights . . ."

"Great!" they all but yelled. "That's it!"

"Don't you want to kick around some other ideas?"

"No," Felix said, shoving some papers toward me. "You're the genius. Draw your ideas and we'll engineer them."

Genius? I thought. No way. *Artist?* Probably not. But for now, who cared?

I picked up a pen and began to sketch.